YEMEN

Jewel of Arabia

YEMEN

Jewel of Arabia

Charles and Patricia Aithie

Interlink Books

For our parents Grace, George, Roy and Eveline

First American edition published in 2009 by

INTERLINK BOOKS
An imprint of Interlink Publishing Group, Inc.
46 Crosby Street, Northampton, Massachusetts 01060
www.interlinkbooks.com

Library of Congress Cataloging-in-Publication Data available
ISBN: 978-1-56656-746-6

Printed and bound in China by SNP Leefung

To request our complete 40-page full-color catalog, please call us toll free at 1-800-238-LINK, visit our website at www.interlinkbooks.com, or send us an e-mail: info@interlinkbooks.com

Half title page, a trader in Beit al-Faqih market carries home his *mada'ah* – water pipe.

Title page, women of the Hadramaut region wear the distinctive tall hats identified with this vast wadi.

This page, typical architecture in Thula displays the intricate windows found throughout Yemen.

Contents

Acknowledgements

We would like to thank the following organisations and people for helping us during the preparation of this work. Firstly, the Arts Council of Wales and the Winston Churchill Memorial Trust, without whose travelling bursaries, much of the initial work could not have been accomplished.

We are grateful for the help given to us by people in Yemen, particularly Universal Travel and Tourism, and Marco Livadiotti and Mahmood Shaibani for supporting our projects in kind. Yemenia Airways helped with air travel and the Taj Sheba Hotel gave hospitality, particularly Vijay Albuquerque and Mathew Kurien. Also Ahmed Abdullah Omer our guide in Socotra and Andrew Grainge manger of Oil Search (Yemen) Ltd.

We would also like to acknowledge the support given to us by the British Yemeni Society, particularly Bill Heber-Percy, Stephen Day, John Shipman and the late Jim Ellis.

Thanks also go to the Embassy of the Republic of Yemen in London, in particular the Ambassador HE Dr Hussein Abdullah al-Amri, as well as the Ministry of Culture and Tourism in Yemen, notably HE Abdul Malek Mansour, and for the assistance of Hisham Ali bin Ali and Atiq Sakarib.

We thank Ahmad Halim for his travelling companionship and spirited assistance and our drivers Naje and Muhammad. At the British Consulate in Aden we received the admirable assistance of Nadir Ali Fazal Ahmed and Mustafa Y Rajamanar.

Thanks must also go to the many Welsh Yemenis who have encouraged and supported us with exhibitions and festivals, particularly Sheik Said Hassan Ismail.

We are indebted to Jenni Spencer Davies and Ralph Turner whose support has allowed us to accomplish more than we could ever have imagined, and the BBC in Wales for supporting projects commissioned by Professor Dai Smith with the assistance of Alison Quinn, and Dafydd Llyr James.

On technical matters we express our thanks to Dr David T Jones of the Termite Research Group at the Natural History Museum in London; Dr E H Arnold, also of the Natural History Museum, for his wealth of knowledge on Agamid lizards; and our dear friend Hagop Karakhanian for sharing his reminiscences of the country with us. We would also like to thank Dr Miranda Morris for her help with the derivation of Socotran place names and Elizabeth Irvine for her kindness and support.

Pat Greetham read the text. Clive Harpwood and Abigail Davies gave us constant advice and inspiration. Sandra Jackaman and Robin Hawkins of the Newport Museum and Art Gallery exhibited our work, and brought it to a wider audience.

Lastly we would like to thank Adele Mutwalli who introduced us to Yemen all those years ago and Hamed bin Hamdan Al-Nahayan who unknowingly funded Pat's first journey to the Yemen two decades ago by his purchase of her paintings.

Our thanks to them all.

CA and PA
November 2008

Introduction

A bedouin wearing a ceremonial *jambia* stands at the south western edge of Rub al Khali.

This book takes the reader on a journey through the country which the Romans called *Arabia Felix* – 'Fertile', or 'Happy' Arabia – capturing a way of life which has changed little over centuries until the 1970s but is now being eroded.

The significant dates in the history of Yemen are set out in the chronology on page xiii. Their confusion reflects the geography and climate of this fascinating place. Myth would have it that the first overlord was Qahtan, an early descendant of Noah, but is silent about where in the country he was established. Archaeology reveals a long history of human habitation on the coasts and in the mountains but most gloriously at Marib on the desert fringe, once known as Saba (Sheba), and for centuries the largest and most predatory of the local states which battened on to the incense trade.

How long the Sabaean kingdom flourished is unclear. The great dam whose remains can still be seen was extensively repaired in the seventh century BC and probably built several centuries earlier. But remains have been found of large-scale irrigation works lower down the wadi over a millennium earlier still. It is now thought that the technology was indigenous, developing first in the highlands where the flows of rainfall were smaller and dealing with greater floods lower down as the technique was perfected. Other massive irrigation works include the ubiquitous cisterns and the regulated 'collection fields', the canals and the tunnels through mountain ridges (through which a bus could be driven) which assured the agricultural prosperity of Baynun. The temples at Marib, now extensively excavated, show a varied and prosperous culture. If its queen did visit Solomon, as the Old Testament says, preceded by a message carried by a hoopoe according to legend (very possibly the royal seal on the letter), then there must have been those at either court who could read each other's script and speak each other's language. Saba must already have been an important state soon after 1000 BC. It clearly sought domination over its neighbours, which included agricultural producers in the temperate regions as well as the service stations along the caravan route. In its final incarnation as the kingdom of Saba and Dhu Rayan with its capital at Zafar, near Yarim, it was still in existence 1,300 years later. But when the dam finally broke, the agriculture which had supported life in this arid place was gone. Why did the dam give way? One legend says enemies released the cats tethered to it which stopped rats destroying the cement compounded with mutton fat with which the rockfill was bound. In any case, the incense trade, which gilded the civilisation, now went by sea and sand covered the region, preserving it for us to wonder at today.

The coastlands, both on the Red Sea and the Indian Ocean, are hot and malarial. There is ample well water, although it is often brackish, and the wadi deltas, to this day issuing from tangled rainforests in their lower courses in places, provide irrigation to some favoured but limited areas. The population shows the results of easy sea communication with Africa on the Red Sea side and with India on the Indian Ocean side. Coastal Yemen was always open to intruders and the signs of their occupation can still be seen in the cities of the plain. In their absence, local dynasties rarely held wide sway or lasted long. Mostly, the more vigorous and prosperous people of the interior controlled the coastal areas.

The highlands of Yemen are said to be one of the few places where the Arabs are at home in a temperate climate. They have always been the source of the majority of the inhabitants of the Arabian peninsula. Many in Yemen believe that most of the Islamic army of conquest was Yemeni. Older people regard the Holy Prophet as 'family' because they claim his mother was Yemeni, and will sometimes refer to him as Muhammad bin Abdullah. The mountains are geologically new; they are steep, rough and intricate. Each fertile valley or run of terraces is separated from its neighbour by passes which a few men could defend against an army. When the Turks attempted to move into the interior from the south in the nineteenth century the watchman at a village in the Qubaita saw the column in the valley thousands of feet below. He threw stones with his sling which hit the column. The Turks thought the village had artillery and they never reached it (the first non-Yemeni did so in 1989). It is plausibly argued that the Himyarites who succeeded the Sabaeans as the most influential political grouping in Yemen were a confederation of baronies, rather than a formal kingdom.

Today's inhabitants in the countryside are still mostly peasants grouped in kinship tribes which in turn adhere to larger tribal federations. The tribal territories have hardly changed for at least a thousand years and guard their crypto-independence jealously. The ruling family of the largest, the Hashid, is called Al-Ahmar. When they are in the present capital people will say 'the Himyar [one plural of Al-Ahmar] are in town' – a sign of the continuity of Yemeni history. Loyalty is to one's tribe and place of origin. It is common for members of the army to take leave to mount private guard on their villages and for workers in the cities to go home for the weekends. In the past the tribal units/baronies fought for sustenance. The rains come each year, but may fall on one village and not another. Then the disadvantaged had to raid for life itself. So each settlement, sited under a rock lip or on a rocky hilltop to conserve farmable land, was constructed as a fortress of vertical farmhouses, each with a wall of loose stones on top for bombarding marauding beasts, animal or human. Unless there was a purely military castle on a neighbouring eminence, the communal grain store – if there was one – was the strongest building of all. Not the least of the achievements of the present regime is to have so enhanced security that no one starves if their rains fail and people have the confidence to build themselves villas away from the ancestral stronghold. But the feuds that the ancient conflicts engendered persist. For instance, that between Dhu Muhammad and Dhu Hussain has been recorded as going on for at least six hundred years – and they belong to the same tribal confederation.

So highland Yemen has probably never been politically united until 1990 save under the rule of invaders, the Ethiopians/Axumites, the Persians (both sixth-seventh century), the early Caliphs (seventh and eighth centuries), the brothers of Saladin (twelfth century), and the Turks (twice, sixteenth and

Right, the Al-Ashrafiya mosque in Taiz was completed in two stages under Ashraf I and later under Ashraf II. In the 1980s it underwent significant restoration.

nineteenth centuries). The Rasulids, who ruled for just over two hundred years after the house of Saladin, and the great Imams who expelled and succeeded the Turks may also have some claim to have done so. But once the Zaidi branch of Shi'a Islam was established in Sadah in the ninth century its influence, spiritual and temporal, spread steadily south until, with the final departure of the Turks, it became the nominal suzerain of the whole of the highlands not under British protection, including the large Sunni community of the Shafei persuasion and other smaller sects. This was made easier by the Zaidi, whose creed descends from the Mutaliqa rationalists and whose law closely resembles the Hanafi, being the Shi'a sect whose tenets most closely approach those of the Sunni. For the rest, the history of the highlands is of the rise and fall of the ruling families of those cities which were both sited at nodal points on communications and dominated sufficient open agricultural land to support imperial visions: Zafar (115 BC to AD 525), Sana'a (repeatedly), Zabid (ninth/tenth centuries), Jiblah (eleventh century), Taiz, (thirteenth to fifteenth centuries) and others. How far their rule extended, whatever their claims, is questionable. Culturally, however, there was a unity deriving, no doubt, from the alternating control of areas over each other from Sabaean times onwards. The customs of the protected people, the classes exempt from feuds because they did a useful job, and of *hijra*, people imported to settle feuds and places where feuds could not be pursued, as well as the concepts of the peace of the Leader used for settling disputes, and of the *rahil*, the human passport, meant that there was contact and kinship between the different elements of the nation. As a result, especially after periods of aggravated strife or foreign domination, a feeling of shared identity could develop alongside the common way of life. This shared identity was carefully nurtured by each liberator and his successors in order to enhance their control and became a powerful popular aspiration. It embraced all areas of what is now Yemen even though some inhabitants had not been within the pale for centuries, and the Mahrah (the area furthest east) and Socotra spoke languages separate from the rest.

Myth has it that soon after the first patriarchs established themselves in Yemen one of the sons split off and made a separate fief in the east. His name, Hadramaut (perhaps a Viking-like kenning, 'deathbringer') still clings to the great valley which is the heart of the Yemeni east. Therein are still served shrines to obscure early allegedly monotheistic prophets such as Hud. The first capital seems to have been at Shabwa where the palace was, according to archaeology, seven stories high when it was finally destroyed by the Sabaeans in the third century AD. There was a dam, although not as impressive as at Marib. No doubt its prosperity was more dependent on the incense trade which passed through on its way from the sea at Qana. Skyscraper cities developed further down the valley and became centres of art and culture in the Middle Ages.

The sea joins and the desert divides. The bare uplands (Jaul) and steep valleys made access to the Indian Ocean easy. Trade with the Orient flourished and, in time, great palaces in mud beside the ancient tower houses reflected the style of India and no doubt the preferences of the trophy wives brought back from Hyderabad. But here too feuds flourished. By the 1920s it was common for families not to be able to leave their house on at least one side for fear of being assassinated from the mansion next door. Well over a thousand agreements had to be negotiated to bring peace to the area.

The modern history of Yemen starts with the revolution of 1962 which, with massive Egyptian participation and after a lengthy civil war, destroyed the millennial Zaidi Imamate and established a republic. As that war ended, the British colony of Aden (established in 1839), the East and West Aden protectorates and the island colonies of Perim and Kamaran became fully independent as a separate republic. (The Kuria Muria Islands opted to join Oman.) The People's Democratic Republic of Yemen (PDRY), as it was known, soon turned very leftist: the northern Yemen Arab Republic (YAR), issue of a typical Yemeni compromise between Saudi-backed royalists and Egyptian-backed republicans, was much more liberal. Although from an early date talks were held about unity, hostility was more common. Two minor wars were fought and an insurrection in the north was mounted from Aden; two YAR Presidents were assassinated. After each event a major step towards unity was taken as part of the solution. The politicians sought both to repair their images, damaged by the insult that disunion brought amid the strong popular feeling on the issue, and to gain, by the terms of the peace, the control over the other party which they had failed to obtain by war. Then, in 1986, a serious internal dispute broke out in the PDRY. The president and a third of the army took refuge in the YAR. When, three years later, the crumbling of the Soviet empire saw support from that quarter withdrawn and the PDRY tried to blackmail the YAR militarily to part with some of its oil revenues, the reply showed that the two states were no longer on an even footing. The fate of Ceausescu in Romania unsettled the leadership of the PDRY, who felt that the alternative to unity was now personal liquidation. The YAR leadership

Above, shepherdesses, fully veiled, with traditional *madhalla* straw hats, tend their flocks in the Wadi Hadramaut area.

Left, decorative houses crown the citadel above Mahwit.

aimed to end the threat to stability for good and to dispose of the PDRY forces by extending control over the semi-independent tribal lands from which many of the recruits in their own army came. Unity was agreed effectively on YAR terms for permanent union, while protecting the PDRY leadership for an interim period. The format was democratic with a free press, multiple parties and a liberal constitution guaranteeing personal property rights. The return of property nationalised in the PDRY began at once.

The YAR authorities held that in Yemen unity was impossible without democracy but that any attempt to break up the union would also amount to an attempt to impose at least partial dictatorship. When the ex-leaders of the PDRY, having lost the election, sought to recreate their ex-state their failure to do so was at least in part due to popular revulsion at the idea of losing these two values, unity and democracy. That the Republic of Yemen survived this rude test in its infancy is why today, as in the mythical days of Qahtan and so rarely since, the land of Yemen is once again united under Yemeni rule.

Mark Marshall
Former British Ambassador in Sana'a

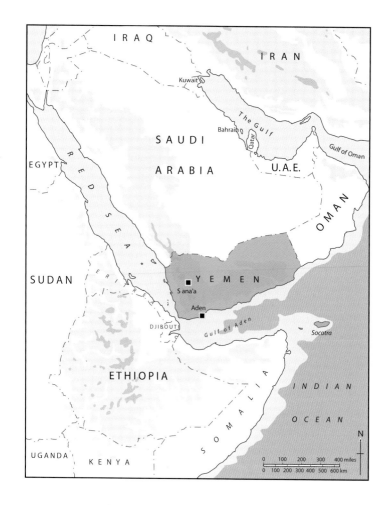

Yemen and her neighbours

Chronology

5000-3000 BC	First traces of Neolithic village settlements in the Yemeni highlands
c. 3000	Bronze Age tools and megalithic structures and agriculture develop in the highlands
c. 2000	First irrigation works in the Wadi Adhana at Marib
c. 1400	Domestication of camel and emergence of South Arabian trading states
c. 1200	Iron Age urban settlement on the edges of the eastern desert during the Iron Age. Beginnings of the kingdom of Saba
c. 965-926	King Solomon rules in Jerusalem. c.960 possible visit of Queen (Bilqis) of Saba (Sheba) to King Solomon as described in the Bible and Qur'an
c. 750	Construction of the Marib Dam. Also palaces, fortifications and temples at Sirwah. Emergence of the South Arabian alphabet. Rise of the rival independent kingdoms of Hadramaut (Shabwa), Ausan (Adan or Aden), Qataban (Timna) and Main (the Minaeans of Wadi Jawf and Baraqish)
c. 500	Height of prosperity and construction in the Sabaean kingdom First rulers known as mukarribs (700-450 BC), later as kings of Saba
c. 300	Greek Empire wanes, Roman Empire now in ascendancy
c. 230-20	King of the Sabaeans conquers Shabwa. Wars of supremacy follow.
c. 115 -109	Emergence of Himyar Federation as rival to Saba as the caravan trade declines in favour of sea trade through the Himyarite ports. Ships begin to use direct route between India and Egypt. Himyarite period – extensive phase of highland terrace construction begins – Himyarite Federation lasts 600 years (115 BC to AD 525)
100	Annexation of Main enlarges Sabaean state
AD 24	Roman Emperor Augustus despatches army under Aelius Gallus but fails to conquer Yemen and Marib
c. 100-200	Sana'a becomes (with Marib) joint royal capital of the Sabaean federation
160-210	Demise of Qataban – annexed by Hadramaut
217-218	Shabwa (capital of Hadramaut) destroyed by Sabaean troops
c. 210-50	Ghumdan Palace constructed in Sana'a
270-280	Himyarites overwhelm Sabaeans
280-295	Himyarites overthrow kingdom of Hadramaut
300	Zafar becomes Himyar capital. Palaces built in Zafar AD 383
c. 340	First documented appearance of Christianity in Yemen. Bishop Theophilus sent by Roman Emperor Constantine II from Socotra to the Himyarite court. Churches built. The Romans and their Christian Ethiopian allies now control the regional sea routes
518	King Dhu Nuwas converted to Judaism
523	Dhu Nuwas declares war on the Abyssinians of South Arabia and their Christian allies. Najran Christians massacred
525	Dhu Nuwas defeated by Abyssinian army under Aryat. Himyarite Federation becomes part of Axumite Empire (525-575)
537	Abyssinian Abraha, Axumite general, assumes government of Yemen
570	Abraha uses elephants in an unsuccessful attack on Mecca
c. 575	Himyarite princes ask Persians to conquer Yemen and expel Abyssinians

575	Axumite rule ends. Persian conquest brings Yemen into the Sassanid Empire for half a century
600	Final bursting and abandonment of the Marib Dam
c. 628	Yemen adopts Islam during lifetime of the Holy Prophet, with the conversion of Badhan, the Persian governor of South Arabia. Arabic supplants earlier South Arabian language
660	'Umayyids in Damascus control Yemen
750	Abbasids of Baghdad rule Yemen
819-1018	Ziyadid dynasty established in the Tihama
c. 847	The first independent local Muslim dynasty, the Bani Yufir, rule from Sana'a
879	Al-Hadi Yahya, first Zaidi Imam, enters Sadah and establishes a dynasty which lasts until 1962
931	Sayyid Ahmad bin Isa al-Muhajir arrives from Iraq. His descendants later accept the Shafa'i rite of Sunnism
945	Al-Hamdani, historian and geographer, dies in Sana'a
1012-1153	The Najahids arrive
1047	Sulaihid dynasty founded by Ali bin Muhammad al-Sulaihi
1069	Sulaimanids occupy northern Tihama coastal plain
1086-1138	Queen Arwa, 'Bilqis the Younger' of the Sulaimanid dynasty, reigns for half a century. Capital moved to Jiblah
1159-1173	Mahdi'ids take control of Zabid and Harad, threatening Sulaimanids
1173	Invasion of Yemen by brothers of Salah al-Din (Saladin) of Egypt. Ayyubid dynasty established (1173-1228). Ayyubids administer most of Hadramaut except Tarim and Shibam (finally captured by Ibn Mahdi in 1219)
1229	Last Ayyubid ruler leaves Taiz for Egypt. Nur Ad Din 'Umar, a Rasulid, proclaims himself Sultan of Yemen. Rasulid dynasty rules Southern Arabia until 1454
1274	Habudis of Zafar conquer Hadramaut (later recaptured by Rasulids)
1298	Marco Polo writes about the ports of Yemen and Socotra
1323/24	Zaidi Imams rule from Sana'a
1328	Battuta passes through Yemen
1454-1517	Period of Tahirid rule in the south
c. 1489	Kathiri Sultans arrive in Hadramaut. Yafa'is from north-east of Aden, invited to assist them, eventually assume control
1513	Portuguese adventurer Albuquerque takes Socotra
1515	Egyptian force beholden to the Turks lands in Yemen
1538	Aden falls to Pasha Al Khadim, commander of Ottoman Sultan Sulaiman the Magnificent's fleet
1538	First Ottoman occupation (until 1630)
1547	Ottomans conquer Sana'a – 1,200 put to the sword
1597-1620	Reign of al-Qasim the Great, an Imam descended from Himyarite rulers. His resistance to the Turks begins the War of Independence
c. 1618	Dutch and British set up permanent factories in Mukha (Mocha)
1635	Zaidi Imams drive out Ottoman Turks. Long rule from Sana'a begins
1600s	Shaharah Bridge built
1720-1740	European trade in Mocha coffee at its height
1728-31	The Sultan of Lahej, a member of the Abdali tribe and a follower of the Shafi'i sect of Islam, declares local independence and takes Aden
1763	German explorer Carsten Niebuhr leads the Danish expedition to Yemen

1798	Britain takes Perim Island
1809	Wahhabi invasion of Hadramaut, desecration of tombs and withdrawal
1830-1858	Kathiri and Qu'aiti Sultanates dispute Shibam – shared administration results
1839	The British under Captain Haines capture Aden as a base for the protection of trade in the Red Sea and as a coaling station. Establish authority locally (until 1967). Egyptians withdraw. Remainder of Yemen under Turkish sovereignty, except for Tihama (under Hussein bin Ali, Sharif of Abu Arish)
1841	Emil Rodiger and Wilhelm Gesenius decipher Sabaean-Himyaritic script
1849	Fighting between Sharif Hussein and the Imam – Turkish expedition defeated
1850	Anarchy in the highlands – Turks maintain foothold on the coast
1853	Aden declared a free port
1869	The Suez Canal opens
c. 1870	First international telegraph station in Aden
1872	Renewed Turkish occupation (until 1918). Sana'a captured
1911	Treaty of Da'an between the Turks and Imam Yahya give him autonomy in the highland Zaidi districts. Turks retain right of appointments in Shafa'i areas
1914	Anglo-Turkish Convention sets the boundary between the Aden Protectorate and Ottoman-controlled Yemen
1914-18	First World War. Imam Yahya supports Ottoman Turks
1918	Ottoman Turks retreat leaving Imams once again rulers of a significant part of Yemen
1918-21	The British occupy port of Hodeidah following the Turkish surrender
1921	Imam takes Hodeidah back from the Idrisi
1923	Turks formally renounce Arabian possessions at Treaty of Lausanne
1934	Treaty of Sana'a between Britain and Yemen formalizes British role in Aden, southern Yemen and islands
1934	Saudi Prince Faisal conquers the Asir Province in Northern Yemen. Province annexed by King Abdul Aziz Ibn Saud
1934	Treaty of Taif (near Hodeidah) cedes Province of Asir to Saudi Arabia
1935	Freya Stark visits Hadramaut
1937	A volcanic eruption in Yemen. Hadramaut alliance with Aden strengthened by treaties with Britain
1944	Poet Muhammad al-Zubayri, 'father of the revolution' in the north returns to Yemen from Egypt, but soon flees to the south to form the 'Free Yemenis'
1945	Yemen joins the Arab League
1947	Yemen admitted to the United Nations
1948	First Yemeni revolution. Imam Yahya assassinated. Succeeded by Imam Ahmad. Capital transferred to Taiz
1950	Anglo-Yemeni conference in London – Anglo-Yemeni Agreement reached
1951-52	American archaeologist Wendell Phillips excavates Marib. Awwam Temple revealed
1952	Imam Ahmad bans ownership of radios in public places
1954	Queen Elizabeth II of Great Britain visits Aden
1954	British Petroleum oil refinery and port opened in Little Aden
1955	First Legislative Council elections in Aden
1955	*Coup d'état* in Taiz, soon after reversed
1957	Visit of Yemeni Crown Prince Badr to London
1958	Yemen aligns itself with Nasserites

1962	Imam Ahmad assassinated
1962	26th September Revolution – army units under Abdullah As Sallal overthrow Crown Prince al-Badr. Civil war between royalists and republicans
1963	National Front for the Liberation of Occupied South Yemen formed
1964	National Front begins Radfan insurrection against British
1965	Organisation for the Liberation of South Yemen (OLOS) and National Front (NF) form FLOSY. NF quits to create National Liberation Front (NLF)
1967	In Aden, British cede independence to elected NLF government. Aden and South Yemen become the People's Democratic Republic of Yemen
1967-75	Suez canal closed
1969	Civil war in north ends. Yemen Arab Republic (YAR) civilian government formed
1969	PDRY President Qahtan ash Sha'bi overthrown by NLF radicals, heralding Marxist rule under Soviet and East German tutelage
1978	Ali Abdullah Saleh becomes President of YAR
1980	Abdul Fattah Ismail removed in PDRY. Muhammad Hassan Ali returns as president
1982	Earthquake in Dhamar claims 1,900 lives. Floods in the PDRY cause serious human and economic damage
1982	Three cites accorded World Heritage status Shibam (1982), Sana'a (1986), and Zabid (1993)
1984	First oil discovered by Yemen Hunt 40km north-east of Marib
1986	President Muhammad of PDRY ousted after heavy fighting takes a third of the PDRY armed forces with him to the YAR
1986	New Marib Dam inaugurated
1989	Canadian Occidental finds oil in Hadramaut
1990	Unification of North Yemen (YAR) and South Yemen (PDRY) to form the Republic of Yemen (ROY) under President Ali Abdullah Saleh
1990-91	Half a million Yemenis expelled from Saudi Arabia under revised immigration rules
1992	Refugees fleeing civil war in neighbouring Somalia begin arriving in Yemen
1993	Elections held under the unity constitution contended by all political parties. Yemen Socialist Party (ex-rulers of PDRY) virtually obliterated. Ali Abdullah Salih re-elected
1994	Brief civil war ensues as ex-PDRY rulers seek to re-establish their secessionist rule. ROY army contingents enter Aden in July. Ali al-Baidh and 7,000 followers flee to Oman
1995	Dispute with Eritrea over the Hanish and Jebel Zuqar islands in southern Red Sea is resolved in 1998 through international arbitration, with the islands ceded to Yemen
2000	Northern border with Saudi Arabia agreed. A suicide attack on the *USS Cole* in Aden kills 17
2001	First elections for local councils held. Consultative Council (upper house of parliament) created. Constitutional reform extends presidential term and powers. President Ali Abdullah Saleh visits Washington in November and pledges full co-operation with the US in the war on terror
2002	The French oil tanker, *Limburg*, is badly damaged in attack off the coast near Mukalla in October. The attack is blamed on al-Qaeda

2003	Yemen holds its third national parliamentary election since the introduction in 1990 of a multiparty democratic system. The General People's Congress (GPC) led by President Saleh wins landslide victory with 238 of the 301 seats. Forty per cent of registered voters are women
2004	Outbreak of conflict between government troops and supporters of dissident cleric Hussein al-Houthi in Sadah province, 250km north of Sana'a. Indian Ocean Tsunami hits the southern coast of Socotra in December inflicting serious damage to the local fishing economy
2006	President Saleh wins another term in elections, extending his 28-year presidency. London conference of multilateral and bilateral donors in November pledges US$4.73 billion to assist Yemen's development. Boat people from Ethiopia and Somalia, escaping famine and civil war, arrive in Yemen in their thousands
2007	Volcano on tiny island Jebel al-Tair ('bird mountain') in the central Red Sea erupts for first time since 1883, killing most of the tiny garrison
2008	Socotra Archipelago added to the UNESCO World Heritage List. Two days of heavy tropical storms in October cause massive flooding, widespread devastation of urban and rural areas, and population displacement in the eastern provinces of Hadramaut and Mahrah. UNESCO World Heritage Site, Shibam, affected

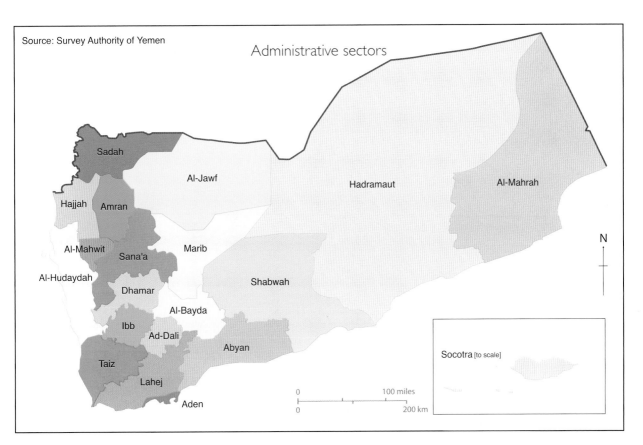

Source: Survey Authority of Yemen

Administrative sectors

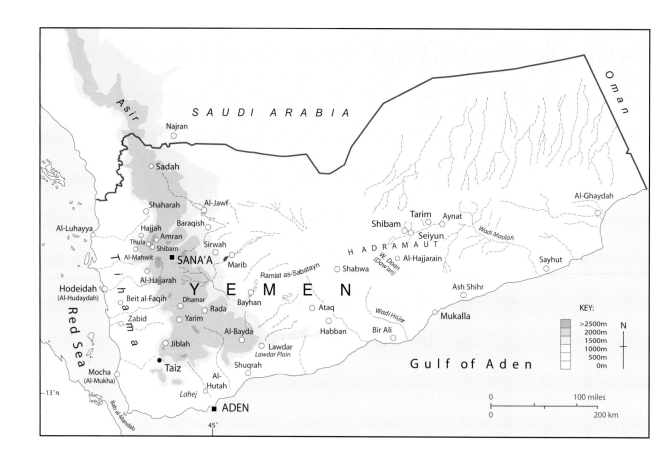

General Topography

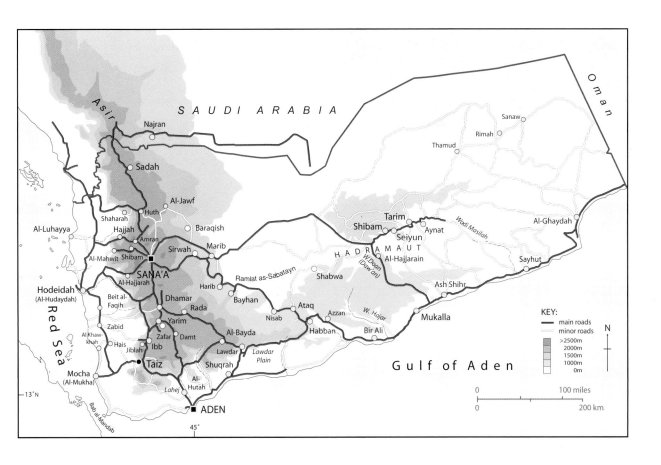

Main Roads

The Highlands

The Roof of Arabia

The rough terrain of the highlands, which has contributed much to the isolation of Yemen's interior, has given rise to unique forms of agriculture, architecture and lifestyle. Until the twentieth century few foreigners saw the area; until the revolution in the 1960s travellers needed permission from the Imam himself to enter it. Those visitors who did travel in the highlands experienced many difficulties and returned with tales of a remote world. But, even though much of the highlands of Yemen is still wild, mysterious and difficult of access, men from its remote villages have themselves often travelled extensively – some, for example, as sailors from the port of Aden during British rule. This has meant that, despite their apparent isolation, many of the people of these areas have a broad knowledge of the world.

Yemen's highlands – which include the Arabian Peninsula's highest mountain, Nabi Shuayb, (3,760 metres) – result from the formation, millions of years ago, of the Great Rift Valley system. They constitute a spectacular upland area which forms the backbone of the Arabian peninsula, along its western edge. The escarpment edge overlooks the coastal strip, continuing south to the Bab Al-Mandab Strait where the island of Perim constitutes a stepping stone between Africa and Asia. Recent volcanic activity has given the region excellent soil fertility. Hot springs occur throughout the highlands and there are occasional earthquakes.

Altitude determines the climate. Although they abut onto some of the world's most arid deserts, the highlands can be very wet and bitterly cold. Rainfall is abundant during spring and summer, and it is not uncommon for two, sometimes three, harvests a year to be produced in the valleys and along mountain ridges. The rugged grey mountains – at first sight apparently abandoned or forbidden by the sun to nurture anything – are suddenly transformed into vibrant green pastures. The beds of limestone and volcanic basalts are spectacularly rich in flora and fauna.

Around these steep and tangled valleys the north-east monsoon winds, blowing in from India, are driven upwards by the terrain, rising and cooling, the moisture they have picked up on their sea crossing condenses and falls as rain in quantities sufficient to support quite extensive agriculture. The area around Taiz and the extensively farmed green province of Ibb has the highest rainfall in the Arabian Peninsula.

The typical community is a village, often based on a family grouping, and adjoining other villages of the same tribe. These are, no doubt, the successors of the Himyarite local baronies under their mukarribs. Each mountain-locked valley has its scatter of hamlets and, more lately, with greater security, of isolated houses. The Yemeni house has been described as a lived-in piece of sculpture. Yemenis are among the world's great builders; nowhere else does the sheer fabric of the local environment present itself so poignantly. The

The road from Amran to Hajjah takes the traveller through the dramatic landscape of Kuhlan, in the Hajjah region, where labour-intensive terracing has made agriculture possible.

1

most impressive and characteristic examples are the multi-storey stone tower houses, most of which are found across the highlands. These are often breathtaking in conception and construction, and their variety is astonishing.

The simplest highland houses are single-storey, but it is common to find both single and multi-storey constructions, normally the work of an incomer or small family, and linked multi-storey blocks forming what in southern France would be called a *bastide*, a defensible community. Each is a vertical farmhouse providing byres, storage for produce, and living accommodation at the minimum expense of precious agricultural land. Often they are decorated either with plaster or by complex stonework. Together they make it seem that every eminence, however slight, is crowned by a fairy fortress.

Unlike the major river-based civilisations of the Middle East, such as Egypt and Mesopotamia, Yemen has no large consistent watercourse. Yet, for thousands of years this has been an agricultural country with sophisticated methods of cultivation and a long tradition of farming skills, particularly in the conservation and irrigation of crops. The East African monsoon rain falling in the early spring (April) and late summer (August) is caught and conserved by a series of man-made terraces, 'hanging gardens' on steep hillsides. Fields trap and use the precious water without allowing it to flow wastefully down the steep mountain slopes. One by one they fill and spread the flow along the contours in a managed fashion. This has facilitated intensive cultivation and prevented hillside erosion. As a result, Yemen has had a settled population of high density for millennia, currently estimated at 42 people per square kilometre.

Yemen is famed for the imaginative decoration with which ambitious multi-storey structures are adorned, in wood, stone or stucco, as here.

The highlands bloom
after the monsoon rains.

Archaeological research makes it evident that terracing has been a fact of life in this area for at least 5,000 years. It spanned the Bronze Age (3000 to 1200 BC), the Iron Age (first millennium BC) and the time of the Sabean Kingdoms, which were followed by another extensive phase of terrace construction in the Himyarite period (115 BC to AD 525). Thousands of terraces have remained intact for centuries. Enormous care and work is entailed in tending the fields. Subsistence agriculture occupies about 85 per cent of highland people. In modern Yemen, most terraced fields are constructed and managed by small household units, which plough, sow, manure, harvest and repair the retaining walls. It probably takes a couple of men about a month or so to build a terraced field of about one hectare (10,000 square metres) using traditional tools. The terraces trap water, intercept run-off and reduce soil erosion. Some fields benefit from the introduction of an impermeable clay layer in the base which holds the water for longer. Nevertheless, some topsoil is inevitably washed off the hillsides and finds its way into the wadis, where it is redistributed down-slope to enrich the fields of the lowlands by as much as 3cm a year.

Up to the mid 1970s, 84 per cent of cultivated land was rain-fed in this way. Since then, migration to the cities and overseas has reduced the workforce on the village terraces, while irrigation from wells has been increasing in the wider plain and valley lands. Yet in the higher escarpment, steep and rocky though it is, the vast proportion of nearly a third of the surface area remains under cultivation. When terraces are abandoned and their walls no longer maintained, the seasonal rains are quick to dislodge the stones and the fields soon

An anvil cloud rises over northern Yemen, sculpted by the high-altitude jet stream.

disintegrate, damaging those below them, so that fertile soil used for generations is washed away down the mountain.

In the past, in nearly every village surface water run-off was collected and stored in cisterns during the rainy season. Many of these works are still in use today. Over the rest of the year remarkably elaborate systems of channels, aqueducts, masonry tanks and reservoirs feed the water to the fields where farmers and local labourers, often women, till the earth. Ploughing on the terraces is traditionally done with a single donkey and a chisel plough; where deeper and heavier furrows are needed on the plains and valley floors spans of oxen are used. Today, tractors are displacing the animals. On the thin, stony soils of northern highland lava fields, piles of basalt along field boundaries built to look like human figures act as scarecrows to deter migrant birds from dropping in to feed. For farmers working on marginal land with thin soil, this can be an essential precaution. The scarecrows are occasionally covered with a headscarf, paper sacks or wigs of dried grass.

Traditionally, highland Yemeni crops have been grains – high altitude wheat, millet, maize, barley and sorghum. Potatoes, carrots, onions, garlic, fenugreek, coffee and grapes also fill many hectares. In the side valleys fruit trees are planted, notably apricots, apples, lemons and almonds. *Qat* (a leaf from a member of the spindle tree family, *Catha edulis,*) which is chewed by Yemenis, has great social importance in the northern regions and recently much land has been devoted to its production. Although its overuse is officially discouraged, many afternoons are spent relaxing, smoking the *mada'ah* or chewing *qat*, while forging and maintaining relationships. The evergreen leaves of *qat*, when masticated, have an amphetamine-like effect. Different varieties induce impotence or priapism, highs or somnolence. Many people's lives are organised around it. The practice plays a part in business as a token of affiliation. Some people regard it as an intellectual stimulant; weighty discussions often ensue. It is purported to increase physical strength and stamina and to improve alertness, to reduce fatigue and promote productivity. Adversely, *qat* can cause insomnia, loss of appetite and psychosis and there

Scarecrows are often made from simple piles of volcanic stone and occasionally draped with material, a headscarf or, more humorously, topped with a wig of dried grass (*below*).

The fecund landscape of Al-Radmah (*right*), on the road from Yarim to Aden, is a testament to the success of traditional agricultural methods.

are those who believe it has other negative physical effects. Moreover, concern is expressed about the amount of family and national resources it consumes.

All sections of society, and both men and women – usually separately – chew *qat*. The seating order at a *qat*-chewing session reflects social status. Each person normally brings his or her own bundle of leaves and lays it out in front of them on the floor. The leaves are bunched in the cheek, and chewing is aided by frequent sips of water. With the juices extracted, the leaves are discarded. News, gossip and jokes are exchanged meanwhile. When a state of *kayf* is attained, with openness and confidence among the participants, discussion focuses on one or two subjects, followed by a quiet mood of reflection as the *qat* runs out.

An early twentieth-century traveller, Hans Helfritz, tells of the origin of the practice:

> A goatherd happened to notice that one of his charges frequently, and for no obvious reason, developed into a state of ecstasy, which caused him to dance about and 'jump over nothing'. The man decided to look into the matter, and he discovered that the goat behaved in this strange manner whenever it made a hearty meal off the leaves of a certain plant. He tried it himself, with the result that it was the goat's turn to smile. He hurried into the neighbouring town, and the first person he met was a literary gentleman to whom he reported his find. The latter went back with the goatherd, sampled the plant, and confirmed that the claims made for it had been in no way exaggerated. With praiseworthy unselfishness, he decided not to keep his knowledge to himself (which showed him to be a true writer). He took a bundle of the leaves back to the town with him, and wrote some very fine verses about 'emerald leaves' and 'the delicious weed'. And so the *qat* habit began in Yemen, in all probability, rather more than four hundred years ago.

Qat plays an important part in social affairs, uniting diverse elements of Yemeni society in relaxation and conversation. A goatherd – such as pictured opposite – is rumoured to be the discoverer of *qat's* special properties.

The highlands of Yemen are home to some of the oldest arable terraces in the world, the centuries-old drystone walls carefully restored after the rains pass (*below*).

The shrub is cultivated in highland plantations, on the wetter or well-irrigated soils between 1,600 and 2,700m. The new, succulent small leaves and shoots are preferred to the large, tougher older leaves. There are pronounced regional differences, due to the type of soil and irrigation techniques: for example, Blue Mountain *qat* from the Shaharah region is so vigorous that it is reported to keep you awake for up to three days. Before the 1970s, *qat* was only consumed

regularly by a minority of wealthy Yemenis, but, since then, there has been something of a boom in *qat*-growing, which is many times more profitable than coffee production. *Qat* is also used in Somalia, Djibouti and northern Kenya and in southern Ethiopia. In some areas the soft stems, rather than the leaves favoured in Yemen, are consumed.

The distribution of food and goods throughout Yemen is managed through a cycle of markets, often named after the days of the week, many of which are known for one craft or product. The more important ones have their own sites but in the smaller villages they are sometimes held beside the road or under awnings in an open space between the houses. They complement the permanent shops in the larger villages and small towns and the *souqs* in the cities. Traders sometimes tour these markets, turning up each day at a different place.

Left, a Stone polisher in Sana'a's old city wears traditional Yemeni dress, including the *jambia* (dagger).

In Yemen, many afternoons are spent relaxing, smoking the *mada'ah* or chewing *qat* – both important social activities.

The *lithma* (*right*) is a large sheet of cotton with bold and distinctive patterning (as *above*) worn by many women in Sana'a.

Sana'a

Sana'a, Yemen's capital city, is a mesmerising place. Its architecture is unique. Tower houses dominate the skyline. Calls to prayer issue forth from ancient brick minarets soaring towards heaven, vying in their elegance and intensity of plea. In the mid-1970s UNESCO declared Sana'a one of the most endangered cities in the world – endangered by redevelopment. In 1986 it was given World Heritage status – a testimony to the importance of its mosques and minarets, schools, *souqs* (markets), *samsarahs* (hostelry-warehouses), palaces, *hammams* (public baths) and the tower houses.

With Jebel Nuqum towering over it, Sana'a sits on the narrowest point of a major mountain plateau, (2,286 metres) above sea level. The region's volcanic origin and regular rainfall make it fertile, and it enjoys a temperate climate throughout the year with the occasional sharp frost in the small hours of winter nights. One legend tells of its founding by Shem the son of Noah. The historian al-Hamdani writes that the Sabaean king Sha'r Awtar built the city wall and the famous Ghumdan Palace (of which, unfortunately, nothing remains today). It is said that Sana'a was also once known as Azal; Yemeni genealogists relate this to the name of Uzal, the sixth son of Joktan (Arabic Qahtan), great-great-grandson of Shem mentioned in Genesis 10:27.

Sana'a has been of great importance since ancient times, an urban centre for the tribes and its market always a trading nucleus for the region. It lies at the intersection of two major ancient trade routes, one of them linking the fertile upland plains, the other Marib and the Red Sea, and was a natural commercial centre. The name Sana'a probably derives from a South Arabian term meaning well fortified. Its Qasr as-Silha, rebuilt on the establishment of Islam, can be seen today with many of its walls still standing. In common with some other places, such as Thula, Sana'a had enjoyed *hijra* status, which is to say that no feud may be pursued within its walls, making them centres for arbitration and peacemaking. Sana'a has also been a major administrative centre, if not the capital, for successive powers in Yemen, be they Sabaean, Himyarite, Abyssinian, Persian, Zaidi or Turkish. It has sheltered worshippers and obeyed rulers of all the major monotheistic religions. While Christianity here did not long survive the advent of Islam, a Jewish presence remained and it has been claimed that until the recent exodus when the State of Israel was established, as much as a fifth of the entire population were Jews. In AD 628 the last Persian viceroy, Badhan, converted to Islam but tolerated other religions; only later did most of the population conform to Islam. Today, Sana'a, whose neighbouring tribes have adhered to Zaidism, has many mosques. The oldest, the Great Mosque, stands on the site of a mosque built around AD 630, during the lifetime of the Prophet Muhammad. It has since been restored many times following floods and wars. Some of its columns are pre-Islamic, some Sabaean and some from the Qalis cathedral, though most of the present structure is twelfth-century. Al-Bakhiliyah mosque, perhaps the most imposing in Sana'a, was built during the first Turkish occupation (1538-1630) and restored in the nineteenth century during the second Ottoman period. Its great domes are obviously of Turkish origin, but the brick minaret is characteristically Yemeni.

There are many gardens in the city. Large garden areas are often sited near mosques, to provide *waqf* (charitable donations for the mosque) by selling

The inhabitants of Sana'a, like the boy (*opposite*) combine western dress with traditional Yemeni attire.

The setting of the old town (*opposite below*) is uncompromisingly traditional, with tall dwellings punctuated by minarets so characteristic of Yemen (*above*).

produce to the local people or into the market. Cultivated gardens and orchards are usually sunk below street level, where earth has been taken to build the upper storeys of nearby houses. They produce vegetables for the market and local families, and are traditionally fertilised with animal and human night-soil. Many smaller gardens, some of them surprisingly spacious, are hidden from view at the backs of houses; they may have terraces that are used for general household chores – cleaning, sweeping, beating carpets, hanging washing and growing herbs. They are playgrounds for the young.

The Old City's dressed stone, hand-made bricks and buildings decorated with an array of gypsum patterns reflect a tradition of urban living which goes back to the Sabaeans and an idea of town planning that is ageless. Sana'a today is undergoing massive changes resulting from rapid development, and the Old City is now surrounded by modern quarters, many of them family groupings, commercial and industrial areas and new suburbs of various social strata. This invasion of the old by the new causes concern as walls and buildings are pulled down and whole areas painted and repaired using more modern materials that jar with the surrounding architecture. Nonetheless, there is hope that conservation can go hand in hand with development, and that one will still be able to walk through large areas of the Old City which seem relatively unchanged from the way they have been for hundreds of years.

Yemen's climate at high altitude gives Sana'a spectacular sunsets (*above*). The city skyline is broken by the minarets of numerous mosques, such as that of Al-Bakirriyah (*left*).

The ancient *souq* (*opposite*), seen from the Bab al-Yemen gate, dates from pre-Islamic times. It is vast and rambling. Throughout its history it has been protected as *haram* – forbidden – to any fighting.

The Ghumdan Palace

The Ghumdan Palace may well have been the outstanding example of the tower house. It was erected in the mid third century on a rocky point to the west of the citadel. Historians describe it as being from seven to ten storeys high (other estimates put its height as twenty storeys) and as being square. Each of its four walls was built of a different coloured stone – black, white, red and green. There was a bronze lion's head on each corner, and the roof was probably alabaster. When birds flew over it, their shadows are said to have been visible on the ceiling from within.

Qalis Cathedral

Christianity was officially recognised around AD 340, when the Roman Emperor Constantine II sent an embassy to strengthen his Himyarite alliance against the Persians and to encourage the building of churches. Under King Dhu Nuwas, a convert to Judaism who was Himyar chieftain between AD 490 and 525, Christians were persecuted, and the Byzantine emperor, unable to act himself at such a distance, requested the King of (Christian) Abyssinia to mount a punitive expedition into Yemen. It was, however, only when the Yemeni lord launched an assault on the Christian principality of Najran to his north and treacherously massacred the inhabitants that the Abyssinians pressed their attack on this mountainous region. By around AD 525 they had taken over.

By AD 537 Abraha the Axumite, an Abyssinian general who had seized supreme power, began building the great cathedral in Sana'a. The city had

Roads in the Sana'a region

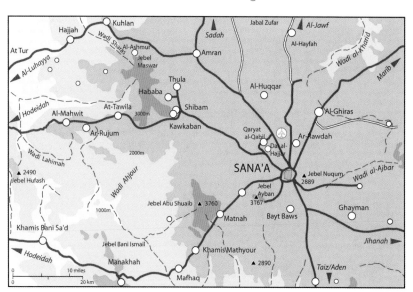

Although much of the Great Mosque (*above, interior, and opposite, exterior*) dates from renovations during the twelfth century, the original building was constructed in the lifetime of the Prophet Muhammad, and parts of it date from even earlier, having been salvaged from the remains of the Qalis cathedral.

acquired pilgrimage status on the grounds of the popular belief that Jesus had prayed there. Abraha was helped by the Byzantine Emperor Justinian I, who supplied materials and artist-craftsmen. The Qalis cathedral, it is recorded, was some 80 metres long and 25 metres wide, with a ceiling of teak, a pulpit of ebony and white ivory, and steps of gold and silver. Marble, mosaic, coloured glass and alabaster were all used in its decoration.

Axumite rule in Yemen was ended around AD 575 by the Persians, who took control for the next half-century. After Islam came to the country, the cathedral and the Ghumdan Palace were destroyed – although the bishopric of Sana'a clung to existence until at least the ninth century. Today, vestiges of the cathedral are few. There was once a large pit which has now been infilled but the layout of nearby houses and streets suggest the dimensions and ground plan which historians describe. Several columns and capitals reused from the cathedral can be seen inside the Great Mosque.

The *Souq*

The heart of the Old City of Sana'a is the large and thriving *souq*, of pre-Islamic origin. It extends from the Bab al-Yemen gate past the Great Mosque. Unlike many other well-known markets in the Middle East, it is open to the sky. The *souq* has traditionally housed forty different crafts and trades. At its hub, traders sell coffee beans and their husks for *gishr*, and raisins, corn and cereals. The spice market is redolent with rich aromas of cinnamon, cumin, cloves, fenugreek and incense. The central part of the market was the Jewish quarter before it was moved to the Bir al-Azab suburb. Its buildings reflect the ancient Jewish prohibition on higher building and none exceeds two storeys. It was called the *Souq al-Milh* (salt market) and this name is now applied to the whole *souq*. It has been a centre for handicraft industries such as jewellery and, most importantly, the making of the south Arabian dagger, the *jambia*. Among other crafts still practised are stone polishing, and the manufacture of blades, as well as leatherwork and carpentry. Each craft had its own guild headman, elected locally to supervise regulations and trade. Other products are brought in from rural areas – hides and skins, silver and pottery from Hais. Cloth from Japan and brassware from India reveal an international trade. In earlier times, such goods came into the city through a *samsarah*: a warehouse and lodging place, which taxed the goods on arrival. The whole *souq* is presided over by the *Sheikh as-Souq*, or master of the market. Another elected official, the *Sheikh al-Layal*, is in charge of security.

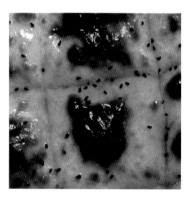

The visitor entering the *souq* for the first time is bombarded by the sounds of traders haggling and craftsmen at work, the scent of spices and herbs and the colour and the delights of the diverse produce on offer: (*left*) Yemeni raisins, grain, honey cake and herbs. Locally crafted brassware, Sadah baskets, *jambias* and local pottery are pictured *below*.

The traders are as colourful as their wares. *Left*, the proprietor of a tobacco stall brews spiced tea and (*right*) the owner of a vegetable stall chews *qat*.

Builders in Yemen never shy away from the complexities of constructing houses capable of being built upon again and again, all using the limited range of local materials. In this Arab Manhattan the individualistic gypsum motifs on the buildings' facades lend distinction. (*left, below* and *opposite*)

The Sana'a Tower House

In the Old City of Sana'a around 14,000 tower houses rise up six (sometimes even nine) storeys high. Many originally had an agricultural vocation limited to adjacent land. The traditional social structures of Yemen partly define the way a house is built. The technique of building combines skill handed down by one generation to another – to produce a creativeness in the use of space and light. While in many other Arab nations houses surround a secluded courtyard and look inwards, Yemeni houses look out on to communal streets.

In Sana'a's Old City a house is typically built on a solid base of roughly-hewn basalt blocks, dug half a metre into the ground, projecting a metre above. The next levels are built of tufa and limestone of various shades, dressed smooth on the outside up to six to ten metres above street level. They are surmounted for the next three to six storeys by burnt clay bricks.

Although the resulting structures may appear fortress-like, much attention is paid to the decoration of the exterior walls and windows, with frequent use of pre-Islamic motifs, including Sabaean script, ancient zigzag symbols of water or snakes, and patterns from intricate jewellery or embroidery all of which often imply some family or tribal identity. Ibex horns, real or figured in cast iron, are frequently placed on the corners of buildings. In Mahwit or Kawkaban, the positioning and colour of the different stones constitute the decoration. Seen at sunrise or dusk, the effect of the white gypsum-saturated wash on Sana'a houses is hypnotic.

Above, the window structure known as a *shubaq*.

One of the most attractive aspects of Yemeni architecture, particularly domestic architecture, is the windows. These often consist of two parts: a lower part, for viewing and ventilation, separated by a lintel from an upper part which serves as a fanlight, filled with alabaster or glass to throw light inside the room. Some windows are simple openings made of shutters, alabaster and stained glass. Others include the *shubaq*, a perforated box structure jutting out from the wall so that a woman can look down into the street below without being seen; similar structures are used for storing earthenware jars to keep drinking water and foodstuffs cool, as they stand in the shade and yet benefit from the breeze coming through the holes. Many houses also have ventilation holes which double as loopholes through which to shoot.

The motifs used for windows have evolved over the centuries. Assemblages of half circles, circles and arches are a pre-Islamic design; others, particularly the rectangular windows and coloured-glass windows, arrived with various conquerors or through foreign influence. The most common in the highlands were round windows glazed with alabaster, which in the warm late-afternoon sun remind one of a honeycomb. Locals often say that these windows create an atmosphere like moonlight, and certainly the natural veins in the alabaster do resemble the patterns on the moon. In later times the brightly coloured *amariyah* or *takrim* windows, with intricate geometrical designs, were introduced by the Ottomans. These are made by spreading gypsum plaster on a wall, smoothing it and drawing patterns on it with a compass which are then cut out before the plaster dries. The window is then taken off the wall and laid flat.

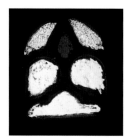

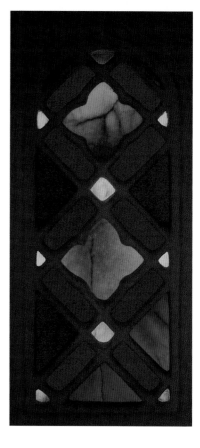

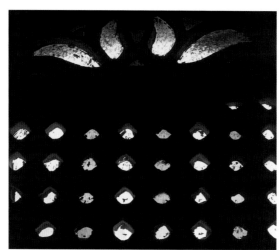

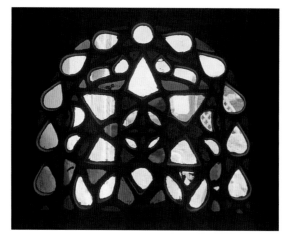

Takrim craftsmen have great scope with which to express their creativity, and their designs vary dramatically. A *takrim*, more than simply a coloured window, is a showpiece, filtering the rays of the shifting sun and casting kaleidoscopic patterns onto the white gypsum walls.

This architectural love affair with light is manifested more simply in the window above the doorway (*right*).

The traditional *diwan* or *mafraj* (*left*) is a place of rest and beauty, enhanced by the stucco gypsum carvings (*below*) and illuminated. by the sun's rays filtering through the locally crafted *takrim* (*above*).

Pieces of glass are shaped to fit, and fixed into the cut-out holes before wet plaster is applied around the edges on the reverse. At night in the Old City of Sana'a such windows are a magnificent sight, casting light and colours out into the city. Inside the house they throw soft patterns onto whitewashed walls from dawn to dusk. In the richer houses *takrims* of different patterns are fitted inside each other so that the coloured patterns on the walls change as the sun goes round.

Inside, if the ground floor is no longer a stable for the cattle it can often be a shop or workshop. The first floor has traditionally been a place of storage for grains; some houses have an old circular millstone, though this is less common today. The domestic rooms usually begin on the second floor, where they are often multi-purpose for sitting, with or without guests, eating and sleeping. The third floor contains the *diwan*, a large room, often running the length of the house, used for grand feasts or special occasions such as weddings, funerals or meetings of tribesmen. Generally the most ornately decorated and beautiful room in the house, it is sometimes kept locked, and opened only for such events. If the house is tall enough, the upper floors, especially the *mafraj* (the main upper room, used mostly by the men for socialising, *qat*-chewing and smoking the *mada'ah* water pipe) may have extraordinary views and decorative plaster reliefs on the walls. These may include shelves as built-in cupboards. The kitchen is positioned high in the house. In Sana'a, kitchens are mostly on the north side, so that the prevailing wind will blow the smoke away.

Washing and toilet facilities are also usually high up in the house, and there will be a stand for a basin with a stepping stone to stand on when pouring water over yourself from a dipper. Liquid and solid waste are separated. The liquid dries as it descends a waterproofed groove in the side of the house, while solid matter goes down a chimney to the excrement room from which

it is collected to be burned as fuel for the *hammams* with the subsequent ash then used as a soil conditioner. The uses of particular rooms change with the time of year. In the winter it can get very cold in the highlands, so the warmest rooms are for sleeping.

Although mud is used in some villages, gypsum has been the traditional source of plaster in many parts of the highlands, being easy to carve and good for covering surfaces. Bathrooms, stairs and hallways are sometimes waterproofed with a mixture of lime plaster, cow grease (tallow) and alabaster powder.

The translucent beauty of alabaster is nowhere more beautifully incorporated into everyday life than in Yemen's traditional homes, as in the windows of a restored house (*bottom right*) and the incense burner silhouetted on a window ledge (*above*).

More primitive structures such as that of the *samsarah* (*right*) – a storage house and hotel for passing traders – uses small open windows, which can also be seen in the kitchen below.

Central Highlands

South-west of Sana'a is Al-Hajjarah, one of the most impressive and easily accessible mountain villages in Yemen. It is situated west of Manakhah, the regional centre of the Jebel Haraz (famous for the beauty of its women). Like so many Yemeni villages, Al-Hajjarah encircles and crowns the summit of a hill. Built of quarried stone from the mountainside nearby – stonecutters still work the mountains here – it looks like a natural outgrowth of the local bedrock. It is a superb example of Yemeni vernacular architecture. The village dates from

The villages of the Haraz region are located and built with defence clearly in mind *(left)*, but the fortified houses are decorated with intricate patterns of white cast on the stonework *(right)*.

the eleventh century. Its fortified houses, made with massive blocks of unmortared stone, cluster to form an uninterrupted rampart. A series of granaries and cisterns have made it possible for this village, like others in the mountains, to withstand a long siege. The fortified houses are highly decorated; some say this is to keep away the flies, others say it is a symbol of having accomplished the *hajj* or marks the room where a child has been born, while still others believe the decorations are protective, like amulets, and have a more ancient pre-Islamic origin.

Nearby, centred around Al-Hotaib, lies one of the Ismaili Shi'ite regions of Yemen. Here, pilgrims congregate from as far afield as India at the tomb of the sixteenth century Yemeni *da'i* or preacher, Hatim Ibn Ibrahim al-Hamdani. The area is famous for its coffee.

Even in Ottoman days, and as far back as the Himyarite kingdom, Manakhah was an important stopping-place for caravans carrying goods from Hodeidah to Sana'a (in fact its name is thought to mean a camping ground). Still an important market town, it lies on a narrow ridge between two mountain areas.

Coffee or *qahwa* was first consumed by the Sufi religious sect, who noticed that it increased alertness during their devotional practices. It then spread

Below this small village in the Haraz (*top left*) the coffee terraces flourish. Lines of coffee bushes, neatly planted on sunbathed south-facing terraces are watered by regular monsoon winds blowing in from India. Bushes are widely spaced to give each plant access to a sufficient water supply although additional irrigation is sometimes needed during the growing season. A surface layer of flat stones or cobbles is often added to reduce water loss.

Above, townspeople relax in the shade of the tall buildings in Al-Hajjarah.

Right, An old man looks out from the window of one of the stone houses in Al-Hajjarah.

Overleaf, Al-Mahwit

among the wider population, although still with ceremonial associations. The popularity of coffee drinking subsequently moved both east and west: to India and Ceylon, across the Middle East to Constantinople with the Ottoman Turks, and on to Europe, where it was embraced with great enthusiasm after the Turkish defeat at the gates of Vienna in 1683. By 1720-40 the European trade in coffee was intense, and it became Yemen's biggest export. Mukha, of course, gave its name to the term 'mocha' for a specific type of coffee.

The coffee that was exported across the world from the port of Mukha was grown in the highlands. Indeed, Yemen was possibly the only place from which it could be obtained in quantity until, by the end of the seventeenth century, bushes and seeds had been smuggled out to Africa, South America and the Dutch East Indies. Tremendous rivalry ensued between Dutch, British and French traders.

Coffea arabica has been cultivated here for over 1,000 years. There are at least six main varieties of plant including Udaini, Dawairi, Tufahi, Bura'ai and Abu Sura. Most resemble the Udaini strain leading to speculation that this variety may well be the oldest local cultivar. Yemen has some superbly aromatic, uniquely flavoured coffees. The best known coffee origins include Harazi, Ismali and Mattari, after their area of origin, and Mocha, named after the Red Sea port, while Sanani is a blend.

Arabica is considered to produce much better coffee than the other commercially grown species *robusta* which originated in West Africa and is still mostly grown there and in Brazil, where it is limited to lower-grade coffee blends as a filler. *Arabica* is characteristically high on flavour and lower in

The coffee bean and the bush on which it grows, *Coffea arabica* (*above*) originated in this corner of Arabia and has only spread to other parts of the world from here, and neighbouring Ethiopia, relatively recently.

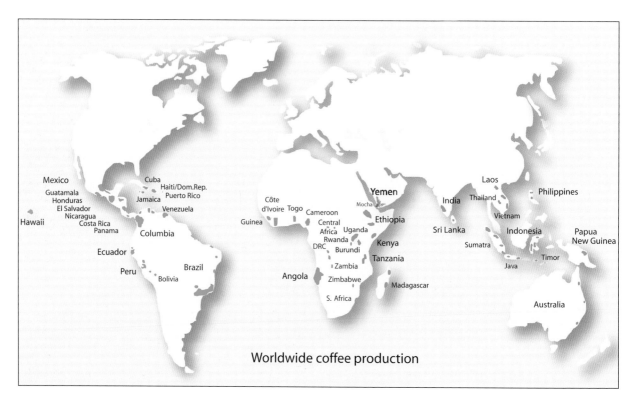

Worldwide coffee production

caffeine and accounts for approximately 70 per cent of the coffee produced in the world today.

Cultivation proceeds much as it has done for centuries. Seedlings grown in nurseries are transplanted to hillside terraces on the high escarpment (the western mountains of Yemen) or to flood-irrigated alluvial fields along the upper wadi bottoms from Rizih, near Sadah in the north, down to Wadi Warazan, south of Taiz. The bushes are planted at altitudes between 1,000 and 2,500m, in regularly spaced lines, irrigated, and protected by large windbreak trees (traditionally *Ficus vasta* and *Cordia abyssinica*), which also provide shade and shelter. Saucers of sugared water are put out to attract bees to pollinate the trees. The dryness of the soil and air in this tropical mountain climate produces a bean which is small and extremely hard.

The best quality coffee is obtained from harvesting the ripe 'cherries'. This gives a good-sized blue-green bean with a dried skin, which produces a good quality *gishr* (a hot caffeine-free infusion of pounded coffee husks, flavoured with ginger, cinnamon and cardamom, much favoured by Yemenis and served to visitors on the conclusion of a meal). Yemeni coffee commands a high premium because of its historic origins and subtle taste, but has been hampered recently by falling production rates caused by competition with *qat*

Highland villagers in the Haraz mountains need to work hard to maintain their system of terraced fields, but their reward is the breathtaking views of the wadi below.

Previous page, Dar al-Hajar is the name given to the rock palace that stands in the village of Souq al-Wadi, in Wadi Dhahr, eleven kilometres to the north-west of Sana'a.

Right and *below*, the methods of farming have changed little over the centuries, with oxen and donkeys sharing the burden of labour, as seen on the road to Shibam.

for acreage and scarce water resources. cf. Giovannucci, (2005). *Qat* is viewed as a short-term source of income, compared with coffee which is regarded as a long-term investment crop. As a consequence, beans are often stored for periods ranging from six months to ten years, as a sort of bank account, to be redeemed when cash is needed. As coffee peaks in flavour and freshness within one year of harvest, this practice of over-ageing results in a loss of essential oils. It is interesting, though, that when the Suez canal first opened and the beans from Mocha started arriving in Europe more quickly and fresher, compared to the longer sea journey around the Cape, they were not universally accepted at first on the grounds of taste as consumers by this time had become used to drinking the aged beans.

All of Yemen's coffees are hand-picked in time, honoured fashion by rural farmers between October and December. Pickers will visit a tree about three to five times in a season. The cherries are then sun-dried for a couple of weeks

In the Wadi Dhahr, a group of relatives are in contemplative mood, with flowers in their headdresses in thanksgiving for natural bounty and the prospect of offspring for the bridal couple. (*below and opposite*)

Tasks such as collecting firewood form a significant part of daily life for women in rural areas. As seen here in the village of Al-Hajjarah (*far opposite*).

on tarpaulins on the roofs of local houses before milling and removal of the husk which is used to make *gishr*.

The beans are then exported worldwide. Today, Hodeidah has taken over most of the maritime trade. Its proximity to the main growing areas, skilled processing facilities, and investment in containerisation makes it a more efficient and lower-cost export hub. Half the crop goes to Saudi Arabia for Turkish coffee whilst Starbucks is the largest single buyer. Other major consumer markets include the United States and Japan, where the coffee is prized for its flavour. From such humble beginnings coffee has grown to become the second-largest-traded commodity in the world after oil.

A few kilometres north-west of Sana'a lies the Wadi Dhahr. A watercourse during the rainy season, it flooded badly in 1975; lives were lost, the local wells were buried and three quarters of the agricultural land was damaged. After this, improvements in flood control were swiftly implemented. Here, in the village of Souq al-Wadi, stands a famous rock palace. Its commanding position and evidence of an ancient well suggest that the site has been used as a lookout post for centuries. It is a classic example of Yemeni architecture and was built in 1786 by Imam Mansour Ali bin Mahdi Abbas; in the 1930s Imam Yahya Hamid al-Din extended it as a summer residence. Nearby is the village of Qaryat al-Qabil, with its walled pathways, orchards, vineyards and *qat* plantations.

Weddings in the Wadi Dhahr are traditionally celebrated on Friday mornings. The festivities often include the *bara*, a tribal dance performed in many areas of Yemen on special occasions. A drummer works up a compulsive rhythm, and local people join in the dance with graceful movements.

The geological story

Columnar jointing in the plateau basalts is a common sight in the early Cenozoic flood basalts of the Yemeni highlands. The basalts erupted en masse through a series of fissures above deep faults between 31.6 and 15 million years ago (Upper Oligocene to Lower Miocene) as the Red Sea opened up and the Arabian plate drifted northwards.

A huge thickness of volcanic rock was extruded, more than 3,000 metres over an area

of 45,000 square kilometres. Early basalt outpourings were eventually followed by massive silicic ignimbrite sheets and minor lava flows. These repeated flows of early basalt erupted at temperatures above 1,000 degrees centigrade, along with copious amounts of steam and carbon dioxide, ponding in vast lava lakes which took tens of years to solidify.

As the lava cooled, contraction and shrinkage occurred resulting in the the formation of joints and the development of regular hexagonal columns, usually vertically within the flow but often oblique near the flow top, as in this picture, (*left*). These are the classic forms of basalts of the Palaeogene in Europe, such as Fingal's Cave on Staffa and the Giant's Causeway in Ireland. The column size depends on the thickness of the original flow and its cooling history. The flat surfaces of the columns are sometimes used by local shepherds as a tablet on which to scratch a grid pattern for a game of draughts.

Marriages are still arranged by the parents when children reach marriageable age. A bride price is arranged; a quarter pays for the party, a quarter equips the new marital home and half buys jewellery for the bride and remains her property always. It is tendered by the groom's father after the formal betrothal, sometimes nowadays in the form of an IOU. This reflects the exorbitant levels of bride price and in some communities a maximum has now been fixed at an affordable level. The wedding itself is a three-day affair beginning with the marriage contract, signed on a Wednesday afternoon in the bride's house. The bride and groom, together with their fathers, take vows in the presence of a *qadi*, an Islamic scholar of the law, who reads the first sura of the Qur'an. In some areas of Yemen the bride's father throws raisins onto the carpet and all those present try to pick up as many as possible as a sign of a happy future for the couple. Money donated by the guests helps to cover the cost of the celebrations.

The main wedding feast is held on the Friday, *Laylat az-Zaffaf*. The groom first visits the mosque around midday, wearing traditional costume and carrying a sword, and is accompanied home by dancing and singing men with drums. Meanwhile, the bride is at her house, dressing and having her hands and feet hennaed while the younger women dance. At sunset the *zaffa*, the wedding procession, takes place. The groom and his relatives parade along the streets to their house. Then the groom runs up to it and jumps across the threshold. Soon the bride arrives with her father, and once inside the house becomes part

Kawkaban is one of the most famous of the highland fortified villages. *Right*, a shepherdess herds her flock through the narrow streets.

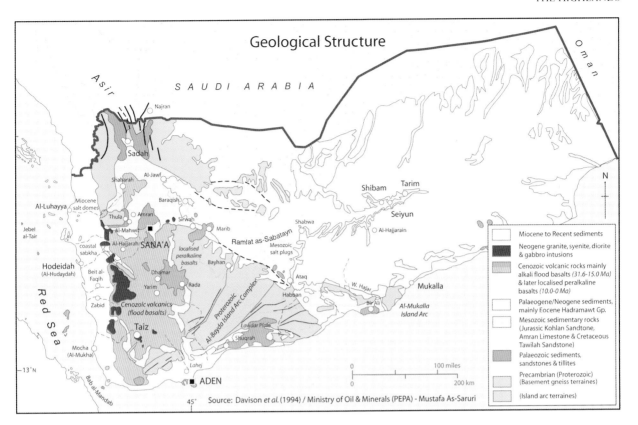

Geological Structure

	Miocene to Recent sediments
	Neogene granite, syenite, diorite & gabbro intusions
	Cenozoic volcanic rocks mainly alkali flood basalts *(31.6-15.0 Ma)* & later localised peralkaline basalts *(10.0-0 Ma)*
	Palaeogene/Neogene sediments, mainly Eocene Hadramawt Gp.
	Mesozoic sedimentary rocks (Jurassic Kohlan Sandtone, Amran Limestone & Cretaceous Tawilah Sandstone)
	Palaeozoic sediments, sandstones & tillites
	Precambrian (Proterozoic) (Basement gneiss terraines)
	(Island arc terraines)

Source: Davison *et al.* (1994) / Ministry of Oil & Minerals (PEPA) - Mustafa As-Saruri

of her husband's family. Celebrations continue within the family circle for a few days afterwards.

Further out to the north-west of Sana'a lies the highland plain of Al-Munakab. It was once densely wooded but is now completely deforested and terraced, supporting a monoculture of rain-fed sorghum. Here are the paired cities of Shibam and Kawkaban sitting above it on a mountain summit. Both are of great age. Shibam is where one of the stories in *The Thousand and One Nights* was based. It has Sabaean inscriptions on its city gate and in the *souq*. The Shibam mosque, one of the oldest in Yemen, is built on the site of an ancient Himyarite temple, blocks from which were reused in its construction. It is famous for the plainsong used in its services. A stairway connecting Shibam to fortified Kawkaban on the peak above is negotiable on foot, donkey or mule, and takes about an hour to climb.

Kawkaban sits on top of a 300-metre pile of sandstone deposited by a vast river system some seventy million years ago and subsequently uplifted and eroded to leave the prominent plateau we see today. This rock supplied the raw material for the construction of Kawkaban with its impressive gateway and wall. It is an ancient site, with a history unravelled in detail by Smith (1982),

Fortified Kawkaban is perched on top of the Shibam plateau (*above*).

The necessity to focus on defence appears not to have blinkered traditional architects to the aesthetics of design. Examples of their attention to detail can be seen in the stonework at Kawkaban (*opposite bottom*).

Opposite above, a shepherd brings the flock home for the night after watering at one of the cisterns on the Shibam plateau. Entrance to this fortified town is gained through an elaborate Turkish gate complex beside the prominent (Al-Qishlah) barracks.

which has ever provided a refuge for the people of Shibam in times of trouble. The narrow chasm separating Kawkaban from the plateau on the Jebel ad Dula side, known as the Qita, is actually a vertical fault. However, the Ayyubid commander Tughtakin, Saladin's brother, partly filled it in with the debris of destroyed houses during his siege of the town at the end of the twelfth century, and stones from the ballistae he used to break the wall can still be seen. After taking the town Tughtakin transformed it with a range of civic improvements.

At the entrance stands the Turkish barracks (Al Qishlah) with its gate complex including Bab al-Hadid or iron gate (actually a wooden gate covered in iron plates). Built in 1895, during the second Turkish occupation of Yemen, it provided modest two-storey accommodation for troops, storerooms and private rooms for the commander. The complex not only guards the approach to the town from outside but was also designed to defend the occupying forces from the town's own citizens.

Inside the town there are some exceptional buildings of beautiful honey-coloured sandstone, which have survived centuries of sieges by Ayyubids, Rasulids and Turks. One is the old mosque, Masjid ash-Sharifah, a name acquired in the eighteenth century from Sharifah Muhsinah bint Abdullah bin Ahmad, but of much older construction, with a striking ablution pool. Built on the centre of the plateau it was originally named after a slave called Sunbul

The cistern at Hababa (*above*) is now a playground for local children.

Settlement perched on a rock above the verdant and fertile valley of Al-Ahjour (*right*).

The town of At-Tawilah (*below*) is characteristic of highland architecture, with its arched windows, its secret cisterns and its flagstoned alleys.

The old mosque of Masjid ash-Sharifah, with a striking ablution pool. Built on the centre of the plateau it was originally named after a slave called Sunbul and contains a prominent Himyaritic stone above the entrance door.

and contains a prominent Himyaritic stone above the entrance door, testifying to the antiquity of the settlement.

Before the Turkish siege and occupation of 1896 there were said to be as many as a thousand very fine houses in Kawkaban. There were also fine mosques and a series of water tanks (Sadd al-Mansurah, Sadd al-Misalah and Sadd al-Hammam) left as a legacy by Tughtakin, underground grain stores (Al Madafin), a Turkish granary (Al Shunah), market buildings, and a prayer ground (the Jabbanah) used for religious feasts. Today there are only some 180 houses left. The population has fluctuated over the ages, through wars and sieges. Most recently, during the revolution of 1962 and as a consequence of the town's allegiance to the royalist cause, many houses were destroyed by artillery and air attack and the more prominent minarets blown up.

Beneath the Kawkaban ridge lies the valley of Al-Ahjour with its splendid waterfall. The buildings in this valley display some remarkable examples of houses clinging on to precarious rock faces. Above the town is a ruined *nuba* watch-tower. *Nubas* are often pre-Islamic structures. They can be seen all over the highlands, and usually hold some strategic position on the border between

The local community thrives chiefly on agriculture.

two tribal areas (for example, on the ridges above Wadi Dhahr and on the road to Sadah, where they protect *qat* fields and vineyards) or double as fortresses. The larger ones are prominently situated to watch out for thieves or raiders over quite large areas. Some have become dwellings or are used as granaries or for general storage. Their structure has influenced other forms of architecture; the minarets and mosques in Huth and Kawkaban, for instance, have a notably similar construction.

Arabia at its most felicitous is represented by the panorama of terraced ridge and verdant valley and the majestic outcrop in the At-Tawilah region (*below and right*).

At-Tawilah, to the west of Shibam, contains a number of beautifully decorated stone houses. Many are built into the actual rock surface, even into old quarries, and therefore harmonise with the landscape to an unusual degree. It has a lively market on Sundays and Wednesdays, held in a market area with unusual stone arches. According to oral tradition, At-Tawilah, like Thula and Sana'a, has *hijra* status, which possibly accounts for the variety of tribal names in the town.

To the north of the Kawkaban plateau lies the walled town of Thula, famous for its decorative round windows and flagstoned streets, which give it an overall urban feeling. The houses of Thula are built of large hewn stone blocks. There are a number of noteworthy cisterns, the best of which is near the south gate, and a Great Mosque with an interesting stone minaret. The whole edifice is overlooked by the ancient fortress of Mutahar Bin Sharaf Uddin, perched high on the adjacent mountain. Thula is also renowned within Yemen for its theological importance, and for its carpets, especially the thick

Above right, a contented male Agamid lizard (*Acanthocercus adramaitana*) defends his territory on a hillside near Mahwit.

In the high, stony reaches, the soil is inhospitable and dry. Here in the 'cloud zone' the *Euphorbia ammak (opposite below)* thrives, absorbing moisture from early morning mists and evening clouds.

kilim, woven from local wool using a sequence of brown, grey and white patterns.

Further west are the magnificent, highly decorative, stone houses of Mahwit, which tower together like the bastions of a great castle. Until the 1970s Mahwit was extremely isolated, with little or no modern development; in fact the road was metalled only a few years ago. Now it is an important market town and, like the region it serves, is expanding quickly. The hillsides in this area, sculpted with terraces which have their origins in antiquity, support the cultivation of coffee, sorghum and *qat*.

On the road north-west out of Sana'a, situated on the fertile agricultural al-Bawn Plain, lies the old walled city of Amran. It still retains much of its ancient stone outer wall. Houses here are built on stone foundations, with stone lower walls and upper floors of mud. The exterior of the windows has a simple plaster surround. Houses generally consist of two or more storeys, with the ground floor used for storage, livestock, equipment and grain, the middle floor also for storage and the top floors containing kitchens, toilets and additional rooms for sleeping, eating and entertainment. The upper rooms are invariably whitewashed and covered in mattresses, rugs or mats.

The main market area (the old *souq*) is along the western wall and is famous in the region for its Friday market. Shopfronts are surrounded by old cylindrical stone columns and simple porticoes. A pre-Islamic past is indicated in the Sabaean inscriptions which are still visible on the main gate of the city and in tablets set into some of the foundation walls and house fronts. The tribe of Amran, affiliated to the Hashid tribal confederation, supported the republicans in the 1960s civil war. As a result, their town suffered very little damage, despite past conflicts with neighbouring villages belonging to the Bakil confederation, who supported the royalists. In recent years the inhabitants of Amran have

been turning away from agriculture and traditional crafts, and migrating to more profitable jobs in the cities.

The drive from Amran west to the old town of Hajjah is spectacular. Built by the Chinese, the route crosses very difficult terrain, where every available fragment of land seems to be terraced, with harvesting often three times a year because of the high rainfall. The road passes the village of Mantaqat Karan, with its round tower, and descends a vertiginous cliff, up which travellers were carried by specially trained donkeys before the age of the motorcar, to reach Kuhlan with its ancient houses on a hillside. Thence it swoops across the valley to reach Hajjah, capital of Hajjah Province. It was once a Zaydi stronghold. During the reign of Imam al-Qasim the Great in the seventeenth century, the tribes around Hajjah and Shaharah held out against the Ottomans as they strove to control Yemen. When Imam Yahya Hamid al-Din was assassinated in 1948, his son Imam Ahmed gathered the northern tribes here to attack Sana'a. Subsequently, he kept his political prisoners in the cells of his impressive Al-Qahira fortress on the hill above the town and many of them have left their mark in the form of poems engraved on its walls. Both the fortress and the Imam's Palace are open to visitors.

The highlanders of the region (*above*) paint their eyelids with antimony (*kohl*) and wear the indigo headdress (*qub*) adorned with fresh herbs.

The *souq* in Mahwit offers a wide variety of goods and produce, like the roasted nuts and incense burners shown above.

Indigo dye is a feature of local fabrics, and dyed cloth is used as a dark base for embroidering women's dresses (*right*).

Northern Highlands

The main road between Sana'a and Sadah passes through a stony, desert-like region scattered with green, irrigated fields with great watchtowers and grain stores dotting the landscape. The tribal centres of this region are Khamir and Huth which, besides having an ancient mosque, boasts an exquisite architectural style of tall buff-coloured limestone tower houses. Leaving the main road here and turning west leads one towards the broad Wadi Lissam with its lush green vegetation and luxuriant plantations of bananas, mangoes and papayas and on towards Shaharah.

Soon after passing Al-Qabai, the famous seventeenth-century bridge comes into view, which joins the Jebel Al-Amir and the Jebel Feesh. This astonishing work was constructed by the architect Salah al-Yaman to connect the settlement of Shaharah with Shaharat al-Fish, on the adjoining mountain. It is built of tough limestone blocks, A cursory glance at the base of the arch reveals the existence of earlier failed attempts to bridge this narrow yet precipitous gap.

The remote stone village of Shaharah, perched at around 2500m on the top of the Jebel Al-Amir, is of ancient origin. It survived heavy bombardment from Egyptian planes during the 1960s civil war. An impregnable stronghold, it enjoys breathtaking views over the surrounding countryside. Women can often be seen sitting balanced on the very edge of the mountain, collecting shrubs for fodder.

Such difficult terrain preserved the whole area from external interference. It was long a royalist, Zaydi stronghold. Imam al-Qasim ibn Muhammad (Qasim the Great) in the early seventeenth century took refuge in the village when under pressure during his struggle against the occupying Turks. Imam Yahya also led a fight from here against the Turks in the twentieth century.

There are 23 cisterns in and around the village. Its architecture is plain, undecorated and ancient-looking. As in most Yemeni houses, the doors open directly onto the street or onto courtyards. They may display intricate carvings or a decorative doorknocker of pre-Islamic form; the Jewish craftsmen who lived in the highlands specialised in these as well as in jewellery. Inside the house will be a spacious but windowless hallway, relieved by a pierced tympanum over the door to let in air and light. The doors are often large, to admit the animals, and sometimes have an inset wicket door for people.

It is proper for a man entering his house, concerned that women from outside his family circle may be visiting, to announce his presence by shouting 'Allah! Allah!', so that they may comport themselves suitably. In much of rural Yemen, in contrast to neighbouring states, contact between unrelated men and women who are close neighbours or from the same village is common and outsiders are not automatically excluded; visiting between women is seen as essential.

North of Huth, the main road towards Sadah continues through Al-Harf, crossing a desolate but beautiful landscape of limestone pavements pierced by volcanic cones. In the mud-walled villages on both sides of the road many of the houses are painted with red ochre stripes, as they are, for example, in Souq al-Inan. Settlements in this area are concentrated where seasonal rains or

The agricultural workload is traditionally shared between the sexes. Shepherdesses are picked out by the setting sun as they drive their sheep up a rocky path in the highlands.

A citizen of Mahwit surveys
the surrounding land.

Shaharah stands at around 3,000
metres above sea level, remote and
impregnable – as was proved when it
withstood bombardment during the
civil war of the 1960s. From this same
stronghold the Imam Yahya led an
assault against the Turks nearly a
hundred years ago.

The streets of Amran (*above and left*) are darkened and kept cool by the high walls on either side.

Above right, a view of the walled town of Amran – one of Yemen's oldest settlements.

All over Yemen, stone shepherd's huts, *saqif*, can be seen in the fields, like those (*right*) on the road north of Sana'a. The huts are used as temporary shelter for the shepherds and their flocks, but are superbly built, with solid vaulted interiors (*above*).

Right, the view from Hajjah reveals the sheer ruggedness of its alpine setting.

Left, a fruit seller on the road to Bajil prises open a papaya to tempt passing travellers.

Right, the highland village of Beit Showta is surrounded by lush, centuries-old terracing, maintained in the traditional style.

Right, a shop keeper in Al-Hajjarah, a small mountain village near Manakhah. Al Hajjarah means, in Arabic, 'the strong one'.

Overleaf, throughout Yemen's turbulent history, the terraced steps and plunging gorges of Hajjah never succumbed to Ottoman rule.

Rural Yemeni women, in their distinctive garb, are seen (*left*) returning to Shaharah with water collected from one of the many cisterns (*bottom left*) crossing Wadi Lissam and (*below*) on the road to Shaharah.

The mountain village of Shaharah, traditionally a Zaydi stronghold, exhibits the architectural style typical of the Yemen highlands.

ground water can sustain cultivation and are traditionally built of *zabur* (layers of coarse clay mud) and *libn* (sun-dried bricks), both derived from the alluvial soil. The houses, many with entrances off enclosed courts, are designed to be defensible and can be used to keep an eye on the fields, like the *nawbs* or watchtowers which double as grain stores.

Overall responsibility for constructing a house is taken by a recognised builder who will have been apprenticed to a master builder for up to ten years. The earth, water and straw are trodden together on site for many hours, then shaped into balls by tossing from hand to hand. Layers are built up on a stone base by a chain of labourers, throwing the mixture from one person to the next, often to the accompaniment of a working song. After being thrown together the clay can be shaped with a flat stick. The colour of the resulting house thus harmonises with the countryside around. Windows are quite small, doors tend to be engraved. Decorative lime parapets and windows are a feature at the top of many houses.

The most common plant in this region is the acacia. This distinctive bush with its deterrent thorns is actually a member of the pea family and has pods. It is much favoured by grazing goats which will even do their best to climb into the trees. Under normal circumstances the acacia will grow to maturity in eighteen years, but with constant nibbling may take up to fifty.

Acacia wood is useful as firewood and is burnt for charcoal. During times of drought the branches are fed to the livestock, inevitably reducing seed production. Uncontrolled grazing by goats destroys the plant cover and inhibits regeneration, with the result that the palatable species disappear and are gradually replaced by less pleasant, even toxic, ones.

The remarkable Shaharah Bridge was
built by architect Saleh al-Yaman, and links
Shaharah with the village of Shaharah al-Fish
across the gorge. Built of limestone blocks,
the base of the arch reveals the existence
of earlier failed attempts to bridge the
narrow, yet precipitous, gap.

Sadah, the most important town in the far north of Yemen, lies only 80 kilometres from the border with Saudi Arabia and was formerly an important centre on the north-south trade route and a place where pilgrims to Mecca frequently gathered. Its ironworks were the source of much of Yemen's weaponry. Its superb enclosing clay walls, still following the sixteenth-century layout, were completely rebuilt in 1992-3.

As a major religious centre, Sadah was the place where the Zaidi dynasty was founded by Yahya ibn Hussain ibn Qasim ar-Rassi, or al-Hadi ila al-Haq (the 'guide to the truth'), a Sharif who came to Sadah from Madina on behalf of the Hamdan tribes to look into the local tribal problems. The region is still known for its fiercely independent tribes. He left, but returned in AD 897, at which time Sadah became the capital of the Zaidi state and the home of the Zaidi Imams. It was an important centre for Zaidi teaching and attracted students from outside Yemen. As Zaidi influence spread, the imams moved their seat to more geographically convenient centres further south; the capital of the last effective Imam being Taiz.

Al-Hadi, the first Zaidi Imam, was buried in the Great Mosque, sometimes called the al-Hadi Mosque in his honour. Much of the building is twelfth-century, and it has an amazing series of domes and ancient tombs. Locals will tell you that the Prophet Muhammad's camel rested here and that a mosque was built on the spot. A walk around the walls of Sadah will provide spectacular views across the city: you can see the twisted alley of the northern Najran gate, where attackers would be repelled by the garrison on the walls on either side before they could even reach the great doors.

Sadah is also known for its jewellery. Yemeni jewellery was rated among the best in the Muslim world and comes from a metalworking tradition which reaches far back into the country's history. This is reflected in the oldest known treatise on techniques for working precious metals, the tenth-century Yemeni scholar al-Hamdani's book on gold and silver. The decline of the craft in recent years is partly due to the emigration of so many of the Jews who practised the craft to Israel in 1948. The surviving Jewish communities live outside Sadah and outside Raydah on the road north from Sana'a.

The combination of gypsum and ochre adornments create a pattern of stripes on the minaret of a Sadah mosque (*above*). The *nawb*, or watchtower (*top*), similar in shape to the minaret, serves as both lookout post and a grain store.

The wild acacia tree (*opposite*) is a goat's staple diet. These agile creatures can climb the branches of the trees in their quest for succulent foliage.

Right and above, Ochre is used throughout the region to decorate the mud brickwork.

Above, a view of Al-Gorza, near Sadah, seen through a window.

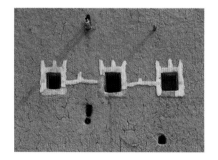

Without their adorned window frames, Yemeni buildings would be little more than drab mud-brick towers. With them, they take on a striking individuality.

The process by which layered mud is built up around the frames with lime and plaster (*zabur*) also serves to strengthen the brickwork and protect it against time and the elements.

The shepherdesses of the Sadah region (*above*) have a haunting call to summon their flocks. Stockades of wild acacia thorns are used to protect valuable fodder from the attentions of hungry sheep.

The peasant tribesmen have always wanted jewellery in the past, but today the urban rich and land-owning sections of society also need jewellery, especially for dowries. Until recently it was common for women to own large amounts of silver. An array of such silverwork for the neck, head, ears, wrists, fingers, waist and ankles was used both for adornment and as a store of wealth, as a sign of status and to mark significant moments in secular and religious life, such as childbirth. Many pieces are heavy (the weight of the silver was the major determinant of value) and they are often further embellished with glass beads, coral, amber and precious or semi-precious stones.

Steatite pots from the Sadah region are commonly found around Yemen and Saudi Arabia and have been traded since antiquity along the caravan routes. Some of the mines which produced them are still in operation today – for example, that at Jebel Razih and the as-Sanad quarry just across the border in Saudi Arabia. Steatite (or soapstone) is a soft rock composed largely of talc that can be cut and shaped into a variety of useful objects, including excellent cooking pots.

Sadah, basking in the evening sun (opposite *bottom*), is the most prominent walled town in the north highlands. The Great Mosque of Sadah (*this page and opposite top*) was built in the twelfth century and is famous for its twelve magnificent cupolas.

Ten kilometres past Sadah on the road to the citadel of Umm Layla is Souq al-Talh, where local produce and goods are sold, together with merchandise brought in from Saudi Arabia. It has been described as the 'smugglers' bazaar' and is well known for its arms market. Women sell beautifully woven coloured baskets here, and there are sections devoted to raisins, *jambias* and salt, as well as, more surprisingly, areas of ground covered in varying sizes of tree trunks brought in from the countryside.

Southern Highlands

The main road from Sana'a to the south divides at Dhamar. One branch continues south to Taiz and Aden, the other runs south-east towards Al-Bayda. Travelling along the latter, one can see, from some distance away, the impressive fortified town of Rada. Rada became the capital of the little-known Tahirid kingdom (1454-1517), which took Aden and Zabid from the once influential and powerful ruling Rasulids who were based in Taiz. Now an important market and administrative centre, the town is famous for its mud-brick citadel (now a jail) and houses, and has an atmosphere all of its own. The Amariya Mosque was built in 1512 or thereabouts in a unique style with no minaret. It stands on a raised platform, revealing a striking *qiblah* and arcaded loggias. The ablution hall has ancient Himyarite columns.

The southern road forks again at Yarim, long an important town, and, passing the ancient Himyarite capital of Dhu Rayan, the eastern road to Dhala and Aden comes to the hot springs of Hammam Damt, 60km south of Dhamar. Here, a feature like a great hollow tree stump rises above the

Baskets (*above and right*) are woven locally and each has its own regional design.

Jewish communities (*top left*) have existed in Yemen since pre-Islamic times.

Women (*below and below right*) not only work in the fields but also make and sell many household items.

surrounding plain surrounded by its lesser brethren. Locally called the 'throne of Bilqis' (an allusion to the fabled Queen of Sheba), it is a recently extinct volcano with a water-filled crater. Since it formed it has been coated in thick calcareous layers of travertine which has been deposited, through heated mineral-rich waters, from the crater bubbling over and evaporating. The rim can be accessed by a series of metal steps. The view from the top is well worth the walk and on the northern slopes there is a *hammam* or spa used by the locals.

Most of the hot springs in Yemen occur in the flood basalt fields on the volcanic highlands where the heat flow is still high, with other thermal springs related to faults along the escarpment and Red Sea margin. The last major volcanic eruption took place in about AD 300. The last serious earthquakes occurred in Dhamar in 1982, when 1,900 people lost their lives, and at Al-Udain (1991) when damage was caused to property. The latter was thought to have been caused by the aborted birth of a volcano. Oil drilling on this side of the Red Sea has encountered very high temperatures quite near the surface and there was a large volcanic event in the 1980s on the African shore opposite, as well as the eruption in December 2007 in the central Red Sea at Jebel al-Tair.

On the Dhamar plateau, south of Yarim, it is not uncommon to see flocks of migratory birds, large and small, accompanied by many raptors. Among them are white storks, *Ciconia ciconia*, which land here attracted by the prospect of food. These large birds need to eat insects en route to keep up their strength. Flocks make use of the rising hot air currents to soar and gain height on the long flight to and from their African breeding grounds. Like many of

Sadah is known for its steatite pots (*opposite top left*) and for the craftsmanship of its silverware, such as the bracelet (*above*) with its distinctive vine motif.

In a country with so many markets, salt has a *souq* of its own, the Souq al-Talh (*right*).

Rada is celebrated for its citadel
(*far left*) and the flair of the design
of its mosque (*left*). For a while,
1454-1517, it was a capital of the
little Tahirid kingdom of Sultan
Abdul Wahab ibn Tahir, from Lahej.

Above locally known as the 'Throne
of Bilqis' (a name for the Queen of
Sheba) Hammam Damt is famed
for its hot springs and towers over
the landscape.

70

the larger migrant species, they choose a route which avoids long sea crossings over the Mediterranean (where there are no thermals), flying via Gibraltar or Turkey and the Middle East, the eastern flocks crossing the Red Sea at the Bab al-Mandab. Most avian migrations are long and exhausting but are brought about by the necessity to survive as winter in Europe approaches, daylight hours become fewer and the food supply gets less plentiful. Well before cold or famine sets in the birds depart for a more agreeable environment to return to Europe once again in the spring, creating the myth of the stork as a bringer of babies – a tradition which links the return of the birds with the fertility of spring.

The Sumara Pass, at 2,800m between Sana'a and Taiz, marks the boundary between the highlands and the midlands. It is a stepped and complex volcanic feature. Here a great deal of effort goes into all-year-round cereal cultivation on terraces. Crops are grown on about 60 per cent of the total cultivated land: mainly *Sorghum bicolor (dhurra)*, with its characteristic goose-neck, with some millet *(dukhn)* and barley grown in areas of lower rainfall or drier soils, together with a little wheat or maize.

The sorghum is used in bread and porridge. Every part of the plant comes in handy. The leaves and stalks provide fodder for sheep, goats and cows, and the roots and stalks are used as fuel in cooking. The ash is then spread on the fields to condition the soil. When the grain is ripe it is cut low to the ground and taken to the local threshing floor where it is left to dry for a week or two before the heads are cut off, threshed and winnowed.

Below, the water-filled crater at Hammam Damt is encrusted in layers of travertine. These carbonate deposits have accumulated over thousands of years. The Damt thermal springs are rich in Na-HCO$_3$ and have a temperature of around 40-45°C, used in the natural healing of ailments such as rheumatism. The source of the carbonate are the underlying sedimentary Amran and Tawilah formations beneath the plateau basalts.

Further south the landscape turns to lush green around the Ibb Basin. Fields of sorghum, millet and *qat* carpet the landscape of this highly fertile region, which has the highest rainfall in Yemen. Ibb sits on a small hill by the western mountains; a typical Yemeni town which over the past fifteen years has exploded in size because of the productivity of the region of which it is the centre and its important position on the road between Taiz and Sana'a.

Some 10km further south towards Taiz, Jiblah (reputedly named after a potter who once worked there) lies in one of the greenest and most beautiful areas of Yemen, at the confluence of two wadis. It was once a wealthy trading town and centre of Islamic teaching, and many of its buildings are three or more centuries old. Its narrow streets are lined with five-storey houses made of the local grey-and-pink-toned stone.

One of Yemen's greatest queens, Arwa bint Ahmad al-Sulayhi (often called Bilqis the Younger) inherited the Sulayhi state from her husband and moved her capital here from Sana'a. Her father-in-law had expounded and spread the Fatimi principles of faith (which belongs to the Ismaili group of Shi'a Islam). The Fatimis educated their daughters, and Queen Arwa was versed in the subtleties of art and literature and a patron of writers and architects. As one writer put it, she ruled by 'wit and diplomacy' rather than by force and brought political stability. She is renowned for investing vast amounts of money in public works and is said to have spent the whole of one year's budget on building and repairing terraces, aqueducts, roads, bridges, markets and mosques, including the eastern wing of the Great Mosque in Sana'a.

White storks, *Ciconia cicinia* (*above*) browse the Dhamar plateau for insects. They breed in Africa and summer in the north, passing through Yemen in the spring. The fertility of Kitab is evident from the face of the landscape (*opposite, below*).

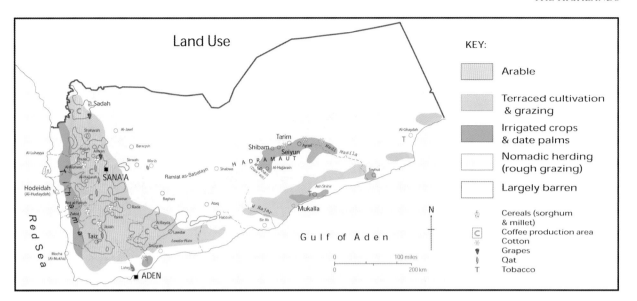

Land Use

KEY:

Arable

Terraced cultivation
& grazing

Irrigated crops
& date palms

Nomadic herding
(rough grazing)

Largely barren

Cereals (sorghum
& millet)
Coffee production area
Cotton
Grapes
Qat
Tobacco

The Sumara Pass at 2,800m
marks the boundary between the
highlands and the midlands (*above*).
Opposite, women work the sorghum
harvest, first by husking and winnowing.
Bread will be made from the flour.

The Queen Arwa Mosque of Jiblah (*top right*) belongs to a town situated in the midst of one of the most fertile – and beautiful – regions of Yemen, at the confluence of two wadis. The queen in question inherited the Sulayhi state, moving her capital from Sana'a to Jiblah during her long reign from 1067 to 1138, dying there at the age of 92.

Above top, the muezzin stands in the doorway of the mosque, while (*above*) a man bathes his feet in the ablution pools.

Left, the Al-Janad Mosque, near Taiz, vies with Sana'a's Great Mosque for the title of oldest mosque in Yemen.

She died in 1138 in her 90s and was buried at the mosque in Jiblah, which bears her name. It is a tranquil place dating from 1088 with a twelfth-century minaret and elegantly designed ablution chambers and pool.

Before reaching Taiz there is an even older mosque, at Al-Janad. Built by a Muslim missionary, Muad bin Jabal, in the early seventh century, during the lifetime of the Prophet Muhammed, it is one of the two oldest mosques in the country. It has been extended and renovated in various ways over the centuries, but the 70m minaret and the ablution pool area outside are original. Qur'anic verses are set into the walls and columns, and, like the Grand Mosque in Sana'a, it has a courtyard surrounded by stone arches supporting galleries.

Today, Al-Janad is a small village, but it is an important place of pilgrimage during the first Friday in the month of Rajab each year. Yet it may have preceded Taiz as an administrative centre as well as a religious one. The shift there probably did not take place until 1174 when Saladin's brother Turanshah al-Ayyubi conquered Zabid and looked to the highlands to the east for a summer retreat to get away from the heat.

Jiblah was once a prosperous trading town and centre of Islamic teaching. Its buildings (*left*) are some of the most ancient to survive in the Arabian Peninsula.

Above, the courtyard and minaret of the Queen Arwa mosque.

Below, A traditional dove painting adorns a rural dwelling.

Taiz

Taiz is a tremendously energetic city. It has been inhabited since pre-Islamic times and has been a capital for various periods during its history. Today it is a centre of modern industry and commerce and buzzes with life. It sits on a plateau about 80km north-east of Mukha at an altitude of 1,400m (4,590ft). The citadel, perched on its own volcanic cone, is tucked under the cliffs of the 3,200m high Jebel Sabr, a granite mountain. During the reign of Imam Ahmad bin Yahya Hamid al-Din, who died in 1962, it housed the hostage relatives by whom he sought to secure the allegiance of the tribal leaders. The city sprawls beneath it.

Taiz lies in the heart of a rich agricultural region where intensive cultivation on terraces takes advantage of torrential summer rains (as much as 63 centimetres of rain falls between April and October), so an abundance of locally grown foodstuffs is always available. Being warmer than Sana'a in the winter and cooler than Aden in the summer, Taiz has long been a place of seasonal refuge, besides acting as an entrepôt for goods arriving from Mukha and Aden en route for the country's interior.

The last Ayyubid ruler left Taiz and returned to Egypt in 1229, leaving in charge a member of the Rasulid tribe, Nur Ad Din 'Umar, who later

proclaimed himself Sultan of Yemen and thus founded the dynasty of Bani Rasul, which ruled from 1229 to 1454. This was a golden period of history for Taiz, during which, as the Rasulid capital, it was an important centre of political power and trade. After a period of eclipse, the Ottoman Turks, arriving in Yemen in 1546, made the city a centre for military sorties into the north and re-established it as a major trade centre, a position it has maintained ever since. The centre of power in Yemen, however, has moved periodically from one place to another, and it was only in this century, during Imam Ahmad's reign (1948-62), that Taiz became the capital again. Imam Ahmad's palace, in Al-Ordhi, is now a museum: a *Marie Celeste*, left much as it was before the 1960s revolution, full of clothes, gifts, watches, perfumes, radios, mirrors and jewellery.

Much of the thirteenth-century wall of the city has disappeared although two of the major gates, Bab Musa and Bab al-Kabir, still remain. The old *souq* is reached through Bab al-Kabir. Although not as impressive as the Sana'a *souq*, it has some interesting goods (many from the Tihama) including baskets, embroidery and pottery and, not least, good and reasonably priced silver shops – probably the best in Yemen. However, the four Rasulid mosques are the city's most important feature. The two finest and oldest are superb examples, Al-Muzaffar, in the centre of the city, and Al-Ashrafiya are named after their

A night street scene of Taiz is pictured *above* and, *below*, a village south of Taiz nestles in the mountainside.

Sprawled around the fringes of the 3,200m Jebel Sabr granite mountain, and crowned with a citadel, old Taiz is being rapidly devoured by modernity. The soaring minaret (*left*) of its Al-Muzaffar mosque was built in the early thirteenth century. It is the oldest mosque in Taiz.

builders, Sultan Muzaffar (1250-95) and Sultans Ashraf I (1295-6) and II (1377-1400). Both are equipped with minarets and built around courtyards with domes, flanked by smaller domes elevated above prayer halls with corbelled stalactite arches. The structures show Turkish–Syrian influence, while the wonderfully decorated interiors and the superb calligraphy that is inscribed therein, recall Persian, Egyptian and even Moorish–Andalusian work. Visually the more interesting of the two is Al-Muzaffar, featuring over twenty white cupolas and dating back to the thirteenth century, making it the oldest mosque in Taiz. However, the Al-Ashrafiya (completed in two stages under Ashraf I and later under Ashraf II and restored in the 1980s) is the more closely related to traditional Yemeni architecture. The most important mosque in Taiz, it has two minarets and a Qur'anic school in an adjacent building. Its elegant plaster decoration and delicate carving display an Egyptian influence, and the great dome of the northern prayer hall is one of the most magnificent artistic achievements in Yemen.

Inside the Al-Ashrafiya Mosque of some seven hundred years ago the splendour still shines forth (*left*). Partially restored in the 1980s, the holy mosque presides over Yemen's most dynamic city.

The Mosque

The first mosques were simple, rectangular stone structures with square open courtyards surrounded by flat-roofed galleries and were built in central positions in villages or towns. The earliest examples, based on the Great Mosque in Mecca, were the Asha'ir mosque in Zabid, Al-Janad near Taiz, the Great Mosque in Sana'a where, in 1972, the oldest known fragments of the Qur'an were found and the Great Mosque of Shibam below Kawkaban.

In smaller villages and towns smaller structures can still be seen, like simple rooms with flat roofs and *shahada* (raised stones in the corners), which add strength to the construction but also echo pre-Islamic use of animal symbolism. Sometimes mosques were positioned on the edge of villages to serve both the community and travellers passing by. Over time, mosques become more complex, the simple prayer hall being supplemented with ablution pools, bathing areas, a minaret, courtyards and a *mihrab* indicating the direction of Mecca. Much of the decoration in these mosques reflects local secular architectural styles, but domed mosques tend to suggest foreign inspiration, including Turkish and Indian – and in the Tihama there is also an African influence. In the cities large mosques were built especially for the *Jami* Friday Prayers at noon.

Decoration in mosques is quiet, although some, like the Al-Ashrafiya in Taiz, have highly decorated shutters, ceilings and windows. In the more important mosques minarets are frequently more elaborate, or higher, and larger mosques have bath houses (*hammam*) for privacy. These are small cubicles for bathing often with their own domed roof. Washing and cleanliness are a very important part of Islamic ritual, and areas where pools, rivers, streams or cisterns exist often become communal areas for gathering – the mosque has traditionally dispensed social services and acted as a place for education, recreation and sharing news as well as reflection and worship.

Above are seen more wonders of the dome, the arches and the screens of Al-Ashrafiya, while (*right*) is seen the grandeur of Al-Muzaffar, the most striking of mosques of the Rasulid period built in the early thirteenth century and comprising over twenty cupolas.

The Tihama

In 1763 the Danish expedition led by German explorer Carsten Niebuhr arrived in Yemen. At that time Al-Luhayya and Mukha were described as the main ports of Tihama, the lowland strip that lies along the Red Sea coast. Since then the coffee trade has declined, and the shift from dhows and fishing boats to modern shipping and oil tankers has seen Hodeidah take over as the main port; the city has seen much expansion in recent years. Yet much of the Tihama beyond Hodeidah is still rooted in the past, and communities have continued to sustain a way of life that has existed for centuries – one unlike that of other parts of Yemen.

The Tihama is an arid zone, where people emerge from the shade into temperatures of 50° C (122° F) and high humidity. Where the small rains visit, unreliably, with the monsoons in early spring and late summer, to produce the distinctive forest communities and lush vegetation we see in the main wadis of Mawr, Surdud, Siham and Zabid. Life is concentrated on the edges – the edges of the foothills, wadis, and coastline, near mangrove swamps, or wherever fresh water can be found.

The bedrock of limestone, recent sediments and basaltic debris from the escarpment have produced habitats that are unique. This coastal strip is an extension of Africa's Great Rift Valley system. Its flora and fauna show many similarities and connexions with those of Africa. It was only about 10,000 years ago that the land bridge between the two continents was submerged. But it is not just nature which reflects an African influence. There is an African flavour about the Tihama's delightfully crafted mud and reed huts and the many unveiled, brightly-dressed women seen in public. African words and accents have pervaded its dialect for centuries. Islam is observed, of course, in Sunni and Shi'ite forms, but the culture also embraces veneration of local non-Islamic saints, the influence of miracle workers, and local doctors performing rites whose origins stretch back into antiquity.

The people of the Tihama mostly fish and farm, though some of them are herders and others produce salt from the salt pans along the coast. In the coastal villages of the Tihama salt pans, called *darah*, are cut out of solid ground and the soil heaped up around them to form barriers. The sea water is channelled in and evaporates, generally over about six months. The pans are then scraped out and the salt piled into heaps. This process has long provided salt for human consumption in the region, with the surplus traded upcountry.

Dates, coconuts and fruit are grown throughout the area, and oranges, plums, papayas, bananas, quinces and lemons on the low-lying lands. Increasingly there are modern complexes and permanent shops, but, as elsewhere in Yemen, there is still a very strong tradition of local markets. Among them are the great market at Beit al-Faqih and the long-standing and frantically busy early morning fish market at Hodeidah with their permanent structures. But temporary markets are also held weekly in many places, it being

Children take an active part in the agricultural life from an early age, and the young folk of the Tihama are no exception.

The market of Al-Maaras is a centre of commercial activity (*left*), but is particularly noted for the quality of its pottery (*above and detail below*), together with the finely woven hats (details shown on opposite page), as worn by this man from Bajil wearing a hat from Abs.

common for wooden branches to prop up stalls made of reeds, straw or hessian cloth or for palm leaves to be strewn across two walls to form a shelter.

Craftsmanship is important in Tihama, too. The marvellous cotton weavers of the region still practise their craft and sell locally. Hat and basket makers abound, often producing work of extraordinary detail, while potters from Hais provide the country with its distinctive glazed earthenware. Throughout the region women can still be found wearing embroidered black cotton dresses with swirling patterns in knotwork that resemble the bright sun. The men dress in white cotton or in a *futa* (Yemeni kilt or sarong) like their highland cousins, but often with a straw hat.

Tihama more than anywhere else in Yemen has absorbed many foreign influences from invaders and traders. The suzerainty of the Imams was often rejected by the sheikhs of Tihama (locals are not Zaidis but have adopted the

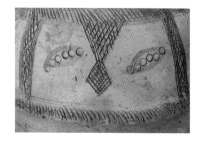

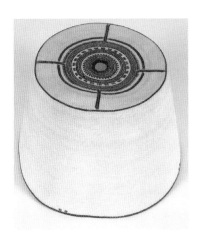

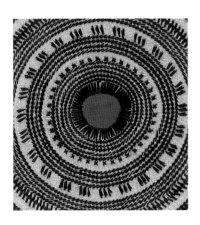

Sunni branch of Islam, and more than 30 per cent are Shafi'i). However, the region was easier to control than the mountainous highlands, and the sheikhs rarely united to ward off an outside threat. In consequence, Tihama was often under the occupation of the rulers of the Asir or of Abu Arish to the north or of the Turks (who built many fortresses in the region) at times when the highlands were in the hands of the Imams.

Most people today agree that Tihama does not end in Yemen but continues northwards into Saudi Arabia. Over the centuries, travellers and explorers assigned it a variety of different boundaries, some extending it as far south as Aden and as far north as Mecca (Niebuhr even suggested that it began at Suez and extended around the whole Peninsula). It is now generally accepted in Yemen as the region along the south-western and southern coasts between Bab al-Mandab and the Saudi border in the north. It is a unique and distinct

place of its own. The region dealt with here – divided at Hodeidah into northern and southern Tihama – is the area within the Republic of Yemen.

Indigenous Architecture

Historically, the highland Yemenis and the occupying Ayyubids, Rasulids, Mamluks and Ottomans have all influenced Tihama architecture, particularly with their religious and military buildings and merchant housing. If there is one main influence, though, it is that of coastal communication with Africa and India. The region's architecture uses local materials, and it conserves and gets the most out of the prevailing hot winds and humid conditions – and in the process achieves great originality.

Unlike the high-rise structures of the highlands, Tihama houses are low. Thatched huts, either circular or oblong, are scattered across the flat coastal plain. Unlike the builders of the northern regions, with their plentiful supplies of stone, Tihama builders take mud, reeds, grasses and palms for their materials (only in some areas, such as Wadi Mawr, is stone used), either using them much as they are, or employing them as the ingredients for bricks (of clay and straw, or clay alone).

From the stifling sands of the Wadi Siham (*left*), a man carries the product of the *doum* palm, from whose leaves will be made the thatched roofs which are such a common feature of shepherds' huts and village dwellings (*top right and bottom*).

Brick and plaster are used extensively in the great Turkish forts at Ad Dahi, Az-Zaydiyah and Al-Mutarid and also in the intricate designs of mosques – for example, in the remaining Rasulid minaret at Al-Mahjam (a mosque described as once having 360 columns and the entire text of the Qur'an displayed upon its walls and columns). Mosques are most commonly built of brick (occasionally stone), whitewashed and have domes.

In Zabid and other towns facades and interiors can be seen where the domestic architecture is extraordinary in its high level of decorative brick and plaster work. In the old coastal Turkish merchant houses coral masonry was used. In the Turkish areas of the major ports, Mukha, Al-Luhayya and Hodeidah, there is wonderfully intricate woodwork and the balconies are of superb craftsmanship. There are many buildings now in poor repair or in ruins which give evidence of a more prosperous past.

The Thatched Hut

The most common type of lowland building is the thatched hut. These are largely rectangular in form, becoming dominantly circular in the midst of the Tihama plain. Their size changes from area to area, and with the needs of a particular family. In some areas they are as large as six metres across. Most are set in a circular compound surrounded by mud walls or thorn, reed or twig fences, or in areas close to the mountains by boulders. Sometimes the cluster includes a few small plaster and coral buildings, a mosque and some trees. One family may occupy a compound of several one-roomed thatched huts.

Although the form and materials may vary, the methods of construction do not. The building process takes about twenty days. It begins with a skeleton made of branches and the boughs of trees, carefully bound together at the top. Depending on the area, either reeds or the hard, dry foliage of the *qadab* bush are woven around this, from both inside and outside. To prevent the wind from blowing the roof off and to increase stability, the whole edifice is tied down using ropes of tightly woven reeds. Mud is often applied to walls and

The picture *above* shows the fine cut of the faces of the young among the people of Tihama. Local craftwork is in evidence in the delicate art of woven grass for thatching (*left*).

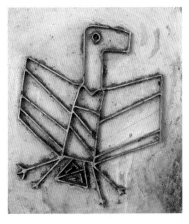

The pictures ranged to the *left* illustrate
the proximity of Africa in the design
of the reed huts, and a rather brilliant
indigenous gift of imaginative
decoration on the interior, as, for
example, in the illustrations of motor
cars and an armoured vehicle from
the Wadi Mawr; and the baubles of
the interior of a reed-thatched hut
at Al-Mutarid.

floors in various thicknesses, inside and out. Together with the thickness of
the roof, this keeps the inside of the house relatively pleasant during the
extreme summer heat. The entrance way and courtyard outside are rammed
mud.

Each hut in the compound is used for a different purpose: living, sleeping
or cooking. Sleeping huts are usually furnished with string beds, positioned in
a breeze to help keep the occupants cool and the mosquitoes from settling.
Kitchen huts have rammed clay stoves and water jars. Inside, hut walls are
often decorated, and mud shelves are built. There are usually straw mats
covering the floor, made of packed earth and these are patterned, with fan-like
designs sometimes pressed into the wet mud. Similar decoration is often
applied to the ceilings, usually by the women, with highly-coloured paints. The
paintings represent the panoply of creation: animals, people, Islamic
inscriptions and everyday objects, including (in recent years) cars, ships and
aeroplanes – even politicians and TV stars occasionally make an appearance.
Wooden pegs are set in rows directly into the ceiling and used to hang enamel
plates, mirrors and woven baskets on. Compounds are naturally extendable.
Unlike the tower houses of the highlands or Hadramaut, where extensions are

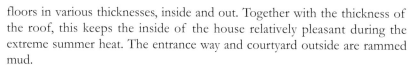

Embroidery on Tihama dress (*above*). On the road to Al-Luhayya (*above right*).

Opposite page (clockwise from top right): brick building, Al-Maaras; Wooden carving in Tihama house; Interior and exterior of a house in Beit al-Faqih; Egrets shelter from a dust storm in the Tihama; Stockaded village near Jebel al-Milh with its round and rectangular thatched huts beside the Wadi Mawr.

Below, Hodeidah is graced with fine examples of elegant residences in the Turkish style – introduced during the Ottoman presence in Yemen.

often built upwards, in Tihama another round hut is built for any additional room required.

Since the straw and foliage woven into the walls of the huts has to be replaced every ten to twenty years the whole hut is usually rebuilt – which explains why so many appear fairly new. In some areas a large proportion of the huts are unoccupied; these are used by migrant labourers searching for work in the wadi zones during harvest time.

The Brick House

The best decorative houses are to be found in Zabid and Beit al-Faqih. The interiors are usually not unlike those of the thatched huts, with visually stunning plasterwork decorated with the same plates and mirrors and household goods and ornaments. The layout of the brick houses is similar to that of the round hut houses, with separate rooms opening off a central space. They are also usually of one storey, although some have two storeys with a staircase and access to a roof terrace. The sitting room often doubles as a bedroom, or a place for chewing *qat*.

The builders of these houses have taken brick decoration to its limit. Many different parts of the building have bricks set at different angles, and there are covering friezes, facades, walls and cornices. Doorways are often highly decorated and in some places show Indian influence. Around Al-Qanawis, Az-Zaydiyah and Ad-Dahi near Wadi Surdud there are examples of brick houses where the bricks have been left exposed, rather than plastered as they are in Zabid.

The Turkish House

Another major form of architecture was brought by the Ottomans. The best examples of the Turkish town house are restricted to the main trading ports.

In Mukha there are a few remains of quite different houses built by the Turkish rulers and merchants. These are made of brick and coral, like the houses found around much of the fringe of the Arabian Peninsula and on the African side of the Red Sea. There remain some good examples in Hodeidah, and some very fine ones in Al-Luhayya, but, as in all Turkish areas in the Tihama, they are collapsing and crumbling at a disturbing rate, and the fine woodwork and carving and painted interiors are fading.

In its organisation of space the Turkish town house is similar to the highland house – hierarchical, but with a business, shop or workspace on the ground floor, though layout varies from house to house. Above is the *divan*, and above that the sleeping area. The internal decoration is often very beautiful, with magnificent stucco work as well as coloured glass, mirrors and paintings. Stained glass is used to great effect. Open roof areas and verandas are common, and wooden balconies are very beautifully carved, as are the windows, doors and lintels.

Hodeidah

Hodeidah is Yemen's fourth city in population terms and certainly the most modern in Tihama. It developed as the leading port of the Ottomans when the coffee trade at Mukha dwindled, and still retains its old Turkish quarter. It grew rapidly as a commercial centre, often in competition with Aden, and in the 1960s was redeveloped by the Soviet Union. Today its centre is packed with goods, cloth, fruit and all the modern extras. At night the markets light up, with men selling fruit under hurricane lamps, and in the early morning the fish market is a hive of activity.

The Red Sea is rich with fish species, and the market bustles as sharks, including hammerheads, rays and yellowfin tuna are carted around in wheelbarrows to waiting vehicles. The smaller fish are often strung together using dune grass. Shellfish are more expensive and less popular, although an abundance of shrimps is brought in, and even the occasional crayfish. Fish are transported into the mountains every morning in galvanized iron tanks on blocks of ice to be eaten fresh in the cities. Others are smoked, frozen or dried, the latter, often sprats or sardines, being made into a spicy tomato sauce. This

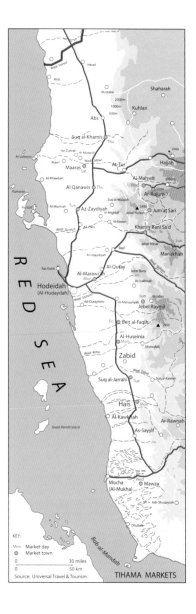

TIHAMA MARKETS

KEY:
Mon Market day
⊙   Market town
0   30 miles
0   50 km
Source: Universal Travel & Tourism

The substantial city of Hodeidah is a major centre for fishing. Its market, illustrated on these pages, serves its own population and a large arc of the western interior.

Opposite, Yellowfin tuna are sold in Hodeidah fish market.

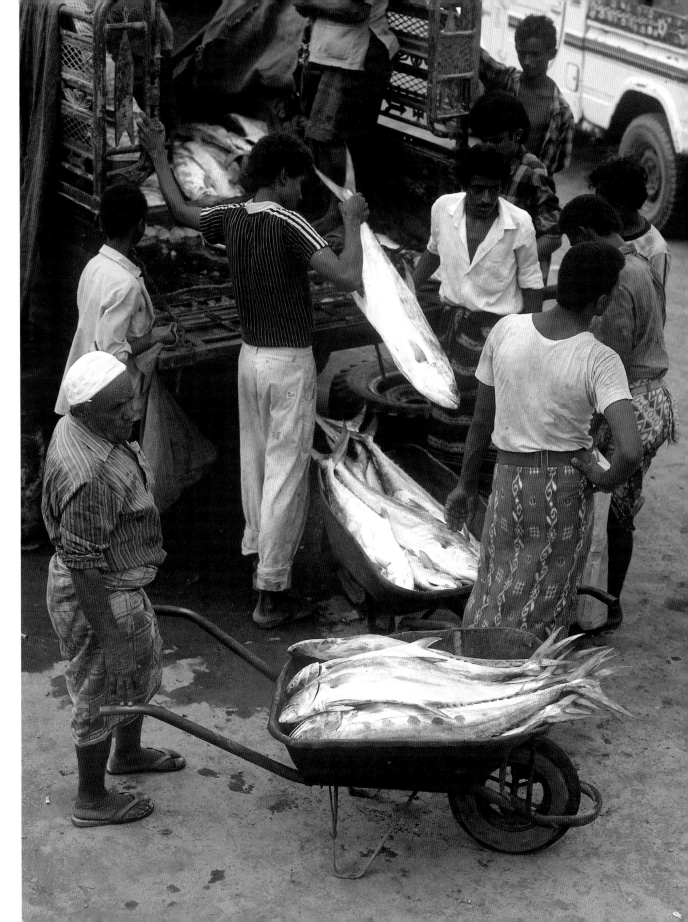

The Red Sea abounds with fish of all kinds. *Opposite*, fishermen unload their boats by the bustling fish market at Hodeidah. *Above*, the prize catch of the day, a giant ray.

sauce is both sold on for general consumption and used with the fresh fish which are baked till black and flaky.

Wealthy merchant families had opulent houses constructed in the Old Turkish area of Hodeidah. Due to neglect, these buildings are decaying severely, but have lavishly decorated plasterwork interiors and superbly carved balconies. Upstairs, decorative stucco work and niches in walls pressed with coloured glass and mirrors scintillate with painted peacock designs – a recurring theme throughout Tihama and an indication of the Indian influences seen in the region as a consequence of sea trade.

Central and Northern Tihama

Inland to the east of Hodeidah lies a remarkable relic of a past age, one of the last vestiges of extensive subtropical forest in the Arabian Peninsula. Apart from the more recent lava flows, sand dunes and salt pans, Yemen was once covered by open woodland and forest. Over millennia, this has been cleared in the pursuit of agriculture, grazing and the endless quest for firewood and timber in a country with an ever-expanding population. The highlands are now completely deforested except for a few woodland relics of juniper in such inhospitable, inaccessible places as Kibbaitah, Jebel Iraf, Halamlam and Jebel Lawz and a few valley bottoms.

The greatest of these survivals covers the rocky granite slopes on the lower escarpment at Jebel Bura. This forest is saved purely by its inhospitability and negligible population. The summertime temperatures, malarial mosquitoes and its position on the border between tribal areas have all contributed to its neglect by man. It is difficult to reach, but may be approached by a lengthy walk from either As-Sukhnah or Souq as-Sabt. Although all the trees suitable for building and timber have long since been thinned, this area represents a unique example of natural, dense, drought-resistant deciduous forest. The south-western slopes of Jebel Bura (2,271m) are clothed with acacia (*A. asak*) and myrrh trees, along

In the Tihama, tobacco leaves are dried for two to three days, ground and used as a snuff mixed with potash. This is usually taken by mouth, but tobacco is also smoked, mixed with sugar and drawn through a waterpipe. The man above, toothless as he is, has also pounded his qat in a wooden container prior to chewing.

Young herdsmen (*top right*) bring the pride of their flock to the meat market, alongside the fish *souq. Above* are pictured details of Hodeidah's houses in the Turkish style.

with some fifty species common in the narrow valleys of the lower escarpment, like *Comberetum molle, Terminalia brownii, Trichilia emetica* and *Phoenix rectilinata* (a palm of the tropical lowlands). In the western valley below, these give way to more riverine forest species, among them *Breonadia salicina* (renowned for its timber), *Pandanus odoratissimus* (the screw pine, remarkable for its beautifully scented flowers) and, again, *Terminalia brownii* and *Phoenix rectilinata*. The forest also contains a stunning fauna of migratory birds and butterflies, hyenas and large troops of baboons; leopards have been seen here quite recently. For fear of the wild beasts, the local people in these mountains insist that travellers may not bivouac outdoors at night and are generous with their hospitality.

A wide range of exotic flora and fauna can be seen in the Tihama. On the dry mountain slopes of the foothills and lower escarpment there is the flowering bottle tree (*Adenium obesum*), with its swollen trunk. This is a member of the dogbane family which has developed into a weird succulent form. As the name suggests most members of the family are poisonous; they yield a milky sap sometimes used as arrow poison – the most severe being the *Somali uabayo*. Reeds are festooned with the nests of the gregarious Rupell's weaver bird. Long-legged hammerkops (*Scopus umbretta*), with their odd-looking head-crests, are more common here than elsewhere in the country and wade in the slow-moving water of the wadis searching for small aquatic invertebrates, often kicking or shuffling their feet to stir up the bottom. These birds build remarkable half-ton communal roofed nests of mud and sticks, up to two metres high, in the forks of waterside trees.

About 50km north east of Hodeidah, the market at Bajil offers a wide range of goods, among them a large variety of woven hats, particularly the *kufia khaizaran*, to protect the head from strong sunlight. The hats made in Abs, further north, are of unparalleled quality with the finest decoration, though cheap copies are also available.

North of Bajil, beside the Wadi Mawr and 20km inland of Al-Luhayya, a group of hills rising in places to 85m above sea level break the flatness of the coastal plain: it is the Jebel al-Milh (or Salt Mountain). During the continental rifting and opening of the Red Sea in the Miocene epoch, seawater trapped in small basins here evaporated and was covered by deposits of sand, silt and gypsum which arched up around salt plugs as they made their way to the surface. Now, on the plain in front of the village of small rectangular thatched huts, the rock salt is quarried in a small open-cast mine in the core of the dome.

Besides Jebel al-Milh, rock salt deposits also outcrop along the Tihama at Jebel Qimmah and four other places. These are of more recent origin (mid–late Miocene) and contain layers of less soluble gypsum and anhydrite; some even form offshore islands, as in the case of Kamaran and the Farsan Islands. On the Al-Salif peninsula salt has been quarried commercially down to a depth of 30m since the 1930s.

Between the fifteenth and nineteenth centuries Al-Luhayya itself was a prosperous port for coffee exports and a landing place for pilgrims going to Mecca. It was here that the Danish expedition to Arabia Felix, led by the German explorer Carsten Niebuhr, landed in 1763. Today it is a small fishing village at the western end of the broad Wadi Mawr, where dhows and boats called *huri* are still made, using a form of rib-and-plank construction. Large pieces of coral from offshore reefs are used in its old Turkish merchant houses, some of which, though decayed, still have the remains of exquisite gypsum decoration – perhaps the best examples anywhere in Yemen.

Southern Tihama

Beit al-Faqih, or 'House of the Sage', was probably named after Ahmed bin Musa bin Ujayl, a late thirteenth-century scholar from Wadi Zabid who settled here after many years of travelling, and whose wisdom was much valued by the local people. Here, some thirty kilometres inland between Hodeidah and Zabid, a huge weekly market is held – perhaps the greatest in the whole of Yemen. It was probably because it was the collecting point for coffee brought down from the Haraz and Mattari regions that it grew so large. Carsten Niebuhr noted that people came from as far as Europe, Morocco, Persia and India to trade here. Nowadays, this market is known particularly for its fine local handicrafts.

There are many deep-fried batter savouries and griddle cakes for sale (these can be found all over the highlands too, but there are some excellent examples in Tihama), as well as scones, muffins, cakes and sesame sweets. Syrup and honey crispies and *halwa* use the honey that has been produced for centuries in Tihama by the ubiquitous bee-keepers.

Palm leaves, reeds, vegetable fibre and grasses are used by women to make many everyday objects that are sold here. Large mats used for roofing and

Pictured *opposite* from the top are the flowering bottle tree, pushing out of the dry ground of the Tihama foothills; then, Ruppell's weaver bird, at work on its nest in the Wadi Surdud; next, the daunting head of the hammerkop; then a kingfisher bides his time in a tree-lined wadi.

Above, fishing boats lie at anchor at Al-Luhayya, on the Red Sea coast.

Map to show the Jebel Bura mountain range

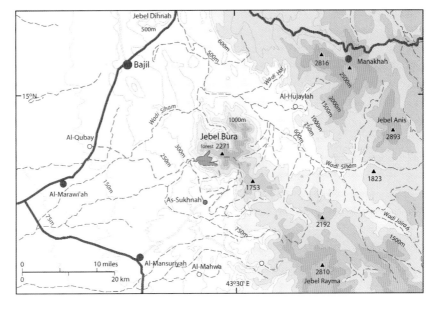

103

house construction, and ropes used in huts, are made from the long coarse grass found along the Wadi Mawr further north. Brushes are often made from bunches of palm leaves or reeds tied tightly together at one end. Many birds are kept in baskets purpose-built for their occupants – whether chickens or pigeons. Muzzles and nosebags are made for camels, donkeys and cows, and plaited baskets of all sizes are produced for carrying larger produce like fish or grain.

Textiles, too, are on sale at Beit al-Faqih. Ancient South Arabia was famed for its textiles. The Old Testament book of Ezekiel mentions 'blue clothes and broidered work' in relation to 'merchants of Sheba'. Indigo was clearly a significant crop in northern Yemen. Even then, surplus plants were exported as far afield as Alexandria. In areas such as the Wadi Hadramaut, where *hawir* (*Indigofera articulata*) is cultivated, it was produced until the early part of the twentieth century and commonly worn by villagers. In the north until the 1962 revolution indigo dyeing was common; the majority of the Yemeni population are said to have possessed some item of clothing made of indigo which had medicinal as well as spiritual importance. It was a symbol of tribal life and was worn by soldiers. Al-Maqdisi in the tenth century wrote, 'There is no indigo

The old walled town of Zabid, seen here at twilight, is now a UNESCO World Heritage Site. The town was once a key centre of commerce along the Tihama's main north-south trade route.

anywhere in the world like the indigo from Zabid.' Carsten Niebuhr of the Danish expedition wrote that he saw over six hundred large vessels for indigo in the Wadi Zabid alone. The last vestiges of indigo production were in Zabid and the Wadi Bayhan, where, until the 1980s, it was the major industry. There are rumours that some houses still produce it, particularly in the Wadi Hadramaut, where items made with indigo cloth can be found in the *souqs*, but the few remaining traders who sell it keep its origin and production a secret. The local trade died out because Yemen opened up to imported clothes.

The warm climate and availability of water in these areas meant that two or three harvests of the indigo shrub could be made each year. Various methods were used to produce the dye. One involved washing the leaves to remove mud, and putting them in tall clay pots full of water, to which other ingredients, including salt, were later added. This was followed by 'whisking' for several hours, foaming the mixture until oxygenation occurred, and then sieving through cotton into a second tub. The small leaves were dried in the sun and pounded into powder, placed in earthen jars with water and left overnight. On settling the dye was taken from the bottom. The cloth was then dropped into the vats of dye followed by further hotter vats which produced a deepening of the colour. The cotton cloth was then hammered repeatedly with wooden mallets until it acquired its famous iridescent metallic shine.

Tradition states that the Prophet Muhammad was clothed in Yemeni garments when he was placed in his tomb, and it has also been written that Yemeni cloth had at times covered the Ka'aba in Mecca. The country's best-known weaving centres have been Beit al-Faqih, Ad-Durayhimi, and Zabid, although there are a number of weavers still working away in their houses in small villages. Traditionally, the local cotton, dyed with vegetable dyes, was used for making cushions, coverings for beds or textiles for wearing as a sarong or a shoulder-cloth, and Tihama cotton was guaranteed by its makers to last at least one hundred years. Today, the cotton and dyes are mainly imported, but the methods of weaving are ancient; it still takes between four and six days to weave a long piece of cloth, one or two for a small piece. The cloth is literally a cloth of many colours, sometimes with a special border with designs passed down within families or neighbourhoods.

Zabid

According to archaeological excavations, Zabid was probably a much larger city in the past than it is now. A magnificent old walled town in a fertile region watered by Wadi Zabid, southern Tihama's major wadi, it lay on the coastal region's main north-south overland trade route, and also had access to Red Sea ports and maritime trade, which brought influences from India, China and East Africa. It was the base for many foreign powers who sought to implant themselves in the region and was seen as a cultural centre during the Rasulid and Tahirid dynasties. The fourteenth-century Arab traveller Ibn Battuta wrote, 'Zabid is after Sana'a the largest and wealthiest town in Yemen.' Today times have changed, and it is a quieter place. Although still an administrative centre for the area, it is not as central to the national economy and politics as it once was. All the same, it takes pride in its rich heritage: its past is still important,

Overleaf, the magnificent disorderly Wadi Mawr drops towards a coastal plain and the sea. A solitary goat, watched over by the goatherd perched on a rocky outcrop gives an impression of the scale.

Left, a father and son relax at their stall in Beit al-Faqih market.

Below, water pots await passing trade at the thriving market in Tihama.

and with eighty or so mosques it retains religious importance. Zabid flourished in the early years of Islam. Its first major blossoming came at the beginning of the ninth century, when the Abbasid governor of Sana'a sent the learned Muhammed bin Ziyad to re-establish law and order and consolidate Abbasid control of the region. Ziyad subsequently founded his own Zaidi kingdom. He set up a university and a series of schools and mosques supported by the religious trust or *waqf*, bringing in prominent teachers of Islamic law and doctrine, including al-Taghlabi, a mufti from Baghdad. Other subjects were also taught, from poetry to history and mathematics. Locals will tell you that elements of algebra were refined, if not discovered, in Zabid. The town eventually became one of the most significant centres of Islamic culture in the region, and an important focus of Shafi'ite learning, so when the Al-Azhar mosque in Cairo opened in AD 971 many scholars from Zabid went to teach there.

Two and a half centuries later the Taiz-based dynasty of the Rasulids (1229-1454) used the city as their winter capital and made its mosque and university a centre not just for Yemen but for Arabia. Some 5,000 students came from a wide area in the Middle East and East Africa to study in Zabid. But in 1538 Suleiman Pasha landed at Mukha with his army and from that seaport established the first Ottoman occupation. This led to the rise of Mukha and the decline of Zabid.

The town has developed a distinctive and colourful baked-brick-and-plaster architectural style which is unique in Yemen. It is laid out in a maze of winding

When this trader at Beit al-Faqih market takes his ease, it may well be with this finely decorated *mada'ah* – water pipe.

streets. It is often said that even Zabidis do not know where to find a house outside their own quarter. High walls conceal beautifully kept decorative houses surrounding courtyards – the most important aspect of a Zabid house -with one or two trees or shrubs (date, lime, fig or basil) planted for shade and ambience. The entrance to the house is via corridors or sometimes a room or two – this prevents accidental encounters between the women of the house and male visitors and ensures privacy. Unlike highland houses, which are often extended to keep members of the family together, most houses in Zabid are quite small. In Zabid, if sons cannot find sufficient living space in the family home they will have to build elsewhere. Today, they will often use breeze blocks and cement, terrible materials in the high summer heat as the rooms never keep cool.

House facades are made of geometrically patterned decorative brickwork and plaster, often deeply incised and always symmetrical, covered in a coating of lime wash, which may be renewed for special occasions such as weddings, births or Ramadan. Inside, beams are decorated with painted flowers and abstract designs, and walls with beautifully carved plasterwork (*naqsh*). The rooms are lavishly adorned with plates, vases, mirrors, photographs and trunks for clothing. The high wooden furniture consists of hemp-strung Tihama beds (which double as couches during the day) with backs often carved and/or painted, and covered with a rich array of cushions and carpets. Besides these furnishings there is invariably a long table in the centre of the room laden with

A great market is not only a commerce of goods, produce and animals, but also of human exchange and lively conversation. (*above and overleaf*).

Dates, cakes and other sweetmeats (pictured here) are all on offer at Beit al-Faqih market.

Above, Al-Maaras market,
Wadi Mawr, Northern Tihama.

Right, thatched hut interior,
Al-Mutarid, Northern Tihama

mada'ah water pipes. Each *murabba'* (long, high room) is occupied by a couple and their children. The family sleeps in this room – or outside in the courtyard during the summer months when the heat is oppressive. Interiors are kept scrupulously clean, which is a remarkable feat considering the heat and dust.

One of Zabid's principal historic buildings is the Al-Nassir citadel built of fired bricks by the Rasulid ruler Nassir Ahmed (reg. 1401-26). There are also many mosques in Zabid, though the most impressive ones are non-Yemeni in origin. The Iskandar mosque, next to the town's main square, can be seen from a long way off, its elegant minaret (built around 1530) and large dome dominating the view of the city. Its architecture shows Egyptian and Turkish influences, and some, pointing to similarities to Rasulid building techniques and floor plans, claim that its architects may have drawn inspiration from them too. The Asha'ir mosque, or the Great Mosque, is the spiritual centre of Zabid. It was built by Muhammad bin Ziyad, credited as the founder of Zabid, in the ninth century on the site of an earlier foundation of the tribal leader Abu Musa bin Asha'ri, sheikh of the Asha'ir tribe in the Wadi Zabid, who returned to Yemen after visiting the Prophet Muhammad and built a mosque near a well in AD 630. Based on the Great Mosque in Mecca, it has a similar simple colonnaded courtyard and a few decorative arches.

Some 35km south of Zabid is the small village of Hais. There are some unique single-storey old Tihama houses with courtyards, but it is the glazed pottery which finds its way into many of the markets of Yemen, for which the village is most famous. The craft dates back to at least the fifth century BC, when there were other pottery-making centres in Tihama. Hais has been producing glazed ware for at least the last four hundred years. Items such as incense-burners, water-carriers and water-pipe bases, cups, coffee-roasters and a great many more utensils are made by local craftsmen and women whose studios and kilns are right next to their living quarters.

The clay is obtained locally and varies in quality but is generally salty and has a natural reddish tinge. Sometimes, straw or even animal hair has been added to it to give the pottery more body and reduce the risk of cracking or shrinkage. All the main techniques are used, including pinching, coiling, moulding and throwing, and gourds are used as formers for the bases of some of the larger vessels. Pots are thrown on foot-operated wheels set up on a stand in the workspace or in a hollow in the ground. The glazed ware is partially covered in a limewash slip and a lead-based glaze, obtained from the electrodes of old car batteries, the various metallic impurities giving a variation in colour from green (copper) through to yellow-red (iron). A variety of decoration is used, mostly abstract but frequently mimicking the design of a woven basket. Larger pots tend to be plain, but the smaller Hais pots are usually decorated, glazed and burnished to increase their ability to hold water. The pots are left to dry quickly outside in the shade of the courtyard before firing in a low-temperature kiln.

Mukha

It is difficult to believe that this small fishing village, with its totem-like remains of Turkish houses and decorative minarets scattered around the Ash Shadhli

Below, Camels while away market day in Beit al-Faqih.

A weaver works at his craft (*right*), and (*top*) that craft on display with the weaver's family at Beit al-Faqih.

mosque in the sweltering heat of southern Tihama was once a major international seaport, yet in the seventeenth and eighteenth centuries it was famous as the centre for exporting coffee grown in the Yemeni highlands (the coffee being given the name Mocha in the west). Looking at this largely silted-up, sand-covered harbour today, it takes some imagination to visualise it as it once was – a sprightly, whitewashed, cosmopolitan city spreading around a crescent-shaped bay, with superb buildings, palaces, mosques, coffee houses, open squares and caravanserais capable of accommodating vast camel trains.

No serious archaeological excavation has been conducted around Mukha, so all that we known of its early history is derived from written evidence. Before the seventeenth century sources are scarce. The anonymous Greek seafarer who wrote *The Periplus of the Erythrean Sea*, probably around AD 100, describes the trade between Egypt and India and mentions the region of 'Mouza', and, of course, Mukha is mentioned by the tenth-century Yemeni historian al-Hamdani. Visiting the port in 1616 on the Nassau, a senior Dutch merchant, Pieter van den Broecke, wrote that the 'famous trading city is adorned with mosques and beautiful houses' and by 1618 the Dutch and British East India Companies had set up permanent 'factories' or trading stations there. The French, Belgians and Danes (and, ultimately, the Americans) followed, as coffee drinking began to spread, and gold and silver poured into the city in payment for the exports. Records of around 1638 show that the population had swelled considerably with the arrival of foreign merchants, frequenting the port with their ships. Early visitors describe camel caravans leaving Mukha laden with goods from as far away as Venice, Hungary and

Above, a shepherd boy takes advantage of the running water to water his flock. *Above left*: a boy from the Tihama, wears a hat typical of the region.

Aleppo in Syria, and goods in transit to other destinations were often transshipped here. Pilgrims en route to Mecca from Oman and East Africa also disembarked at the port. In its heyday, Mukha was truly a melting pot for peoples and cultures from all around the world. In 1696 an English clergyman John Ovington described it as 'the principal port' in the Red Sea area, and in 1763 Carsten Niebuhr wrote of its splendid houses, date palms and 'lovely gardens'.

The early seventeenth-century history of this enigmatic city has recently been painstakingly reconstructed by C G Brouwer, using Dutch East India Company records. He conjures up an intriguing picture. Dominating the centre of the harbour front was an impressive governor's palace flanked by the Great Friday Mosque (still seen today) with its imposing minaret used by sailors as a navigation mark as they made for harbour. Beside the central jetty were a weighing house, a toll house for the payment of import-export duties, and

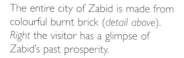
The entire city of Zabid is made from colourful burnt brick (*detail above*). *Right* the visitor has a glimpse of Zabid's past prosperity.

The interiors of the fine houses of Zabid (*above left*) are exquisitely decorated with flower and abstract designs and moulded plasterwork. The exteriors have acquired dignity.

The spiritual centre of Zabid is the Asha'ir Mosque, whose interior is seen (*opposite right*).

Above, the Iskandar (Alexander) Mosque rises with dignified assurance.

Hais is a pottery centre, and its wares and one of its potters are illustrated on these pages.

warehouses. As the bay was only about three fathoms (5.5m) deep, smaller shallow-draft boats transported goods and people to and from the ocean-going vessels in the bay. Also close to the waterfront were lodging houses and hotels for sailors and captains, and trading posts, 'factories', for the transaction of commerce. In the market, produce brought in by pack animals from the surrounding countryside was sold to provision the thriving international port, and there were large numbers of flat-roofed merchants' and administrators' houses built of stone and brick, as well as smaller rectangular mud-and-reed houses of Tihama style strung out around the bay on the outskirts of town.

The city of Mukha (*right*) was once the world's centre for the export of coffee. Its days of glory three centuries ago are reflected in its sacred buildings seen, *opposite*, both restored and awaiting restoration.

There was great pomp and ceremony attached to arrivals and departures in the harbour. It was a port regulation of the period that newly arrived vessels had to be inspected by the port authority and had to surrender their sails and rudder. Those whose presence was unwelcome were denied provisioning, with dire consequences for health and discipline on board. Ship movements were governed by the arrival of the monsoon winds, with ships commonly lying at anchor in the port for months. The main drawbacks to port life were scarcity of firewood for cooking and of suitable drinking water. Both were enormously expensive. Ships from Europe arrived during the spring and summer months and departed in the autumn or winter.

The Hadramaut,
South Coast & Aden

The Hadramaut

The people of Hadramaut, so they maintain, are descended from a chieftain of that name who was the son of Qahtan, a direct descendant of Noah. This relationship, with the two names in Hebrew form, appears in the Old Testament of the Bible. Tribal names in Arabia tend to hark back to an eponymous and mythical ancestor so there could have been a tribe of that name settled here, although the word Hadramaut has meanings which seem more like a nickname than a proper name. Indeed, it is sometimes suggested that it signifies 'deathbringer', a reference to its bearer's lethality on the battlefield, or perhaps it comes from the ancient Arabic for a place of settlement of the dead. Legends maintain that Hadramaut's history begins with the Flood and that the area was inhabited by giants. Archaeologists, who have collected flint chippings, know that it has been inhabited since the Stone Age and that, later, due to elaborate irrigation systems, the land was covered with green vegetation, groves and trees. Whatever its origins, the area, together with the south coast and Aden, constitutes one of the great and extraordinary regions of Yemen.

Although the exact boundaries of Hadramaut are still debated, it covers an extensive area of varied landscape, from the coastlands of the Indian Ocean, through a complex series of valleys, to the southern edge of the Rub al-Khali desert. It includes a massive and magnificent wadi system, one of the largest in the Arabian Peninsula, which runs for nearly 160km from west to east with numerous tributary valleys, such as Wadi Doan, Amd, Al-'Ain, Sakr, Bin Ali, and Idm, and an easterly extension into the less fertile Wadi Masilah. The system is protected behind a mountainous plateau known locally as the Jaul. This desolate and sometimes arid plateau, through which the wadi systems have cut, has little or no dependable water – that is, until you reach the eastern regions, where sparse rain and periodic flooding have seeped into an aquifer, which can be tapped. Living in an area of little rainfall, the inhabitants of Hadramaut have developed sophisticated methods of land use since earliest times. Irrigation, both by control of the twice yearly seasonal floods and, especially, from wells, is carefully managed. Largely based on oasis cultivation, vast areas of date-palm trees grow alongside basic wheats, vegetables, dates and tobacco. This is typical of the significant areas of agricultural development around Shibam – believed by many scholars to be the place to which the people of Shabwa fled when their city was destroyed – other major settlements in the Wadi include Seiyun and Tarim.

Historically, Hadramis have been great travellers, journeying extensively to the east coast of Africa, the Indian subcontinent and South East Asia to make their fortunes in trade and business, and Mukalla remains a busy port to this day.

Parts of Hadramaut catch dependable rains, replenishing the oases and providing crops such as the field of alfalfa (left), worked by the village women draped with the utmost modesty.

Right, a Yemeni woman, clad in the traditional *niqaab* passes through a side street in Shibam

The *madhalla* straw hat is the universal characteristic of womenfolk in and around the Wadi Hadramaut, seen in these pictures and *overleaf* with their animals – goats, sheep and donkeys – on which life depends.

It is not unusual to hear Hadramis talk of the area as if it were a distinct country in its own right. Indeed, isolated within their great wadis Hadramis have developed a unique, almost timeless culture. This is expressed in extraordinary architectural styles, accentuating sheer spaciousness and simple forms. The buildings fuse almost imperceptibly into the landscape; there is a sense of space, emptiness and a dramatic relationship of parts of buildings with the whole and of buildings with each other

Ancient inscriptions relating to the region's long history are scattered across the land. We know that some of its towns are among the longest-settled in the Arab world and enjoyed a high level of culture. When the camel was domesticated in the latter part of the second millennium BC there is believed to have been a trade route between Hadramaut and Babylon, and later there were caravan and sea connections with Syria and Palestine. Archaeological evidence shows that the peoples living here were well established when Saba was flourishing and traded both with that kingdom and with Qataban and Main. The nomads in the desert areas and fishermen on the coast were in contact with other north Arabian tribes and peoples.

Right, the Wadi Hadramaut drains
a vast region of surrounding uplands,
shedding water into the Ramlat
as-Sabatayn

Left, the road to Shibam. Villages nestle
beneath the escarpment so as to not
infringe on valuable agricultural land.

Incense

Incense covers a whole range of gums, resins and spices which perfume a
space when burned or when they evaporate. Frankincense and myrrh are
gum resins obtained by cutting and peeling several centimetres off the bark
of small trees during the summer months. Frankincense comes from trees
of the genus *Boswellia* (named after James Boswell, the biographer of Dr
Samuel Johnson), which grows at an altitude of around 650m in subtropical
regions. They have an ash-coloured trunk, and their lower branches are close
to the ground. Cuts made into the stem during the summer months produce
a green transparent gum, which hardens and is then collected in the autumn.
Boswellia trees also grow in Dhofar (now in modern-day Oman), but evidence
suggests that their cultivation there developed long after the trees became
established in the Wadi Hadramaut; the author of *The Periplus of the Erythrean
Sea* says that the 'Hadrami people alone and no other people among the
Arabians behold the incense tree'. Myrrh trees (*Commiphora* or *Balsamodendron
myrrha*), grown in northern Yemen, exude a bitter and transparent aromatic
gum from the bark when it is cut; this, too, hardens and is collected later.

The frankincense trade was dominated by various states controlling the
trade routes and areas of cultivation. Incense, brought from abroad or gathered
in Hadramaut, Dhofar or even Somalia, was taken by camel caravans to
northern Arabia, the Gulf and the Mediterranean. There was great demand
from ancient Egypt for frankincense, myrrh and spices, which were needed
for burials, and almost all the other ancient civilisations used incense in their
ceremonies. Today, incenses, like myrrh, are still used as a base for perfumes
and also in medicinal applications. In many households in the Arabian
Peninsula visitors are invited to waft the smoke from an incense-burner over
and under their clothes after a meal and then to sprinkle themselves
with perfume.

Mahrah was a major producer of frankincense, as was Dhofar, whence the main routes came overland to Shabwa, the ancient capital of Hadramaut, and also, later on, by sea along the coast to Qana (now Bir Ali). From there, they led north by a track known as the 'gold and incense road'. The camels, which used to transport the goods from about the fifteenth century BC, were able to work very long hours and needed little water. They could make the 60–70 day journey through southern Arabia to Mecca and on, via Petra to Gaza. Camel caravans grew to two or three thousand strong; and garrisons were established to ensure their security in towns along their route: Yathrib (now Madina) was one.

Apart from dealing in frankincense and myrrh, mining and trading gold, silver, lead, copper, zinc and iron were actively pursued in Yemen long before the arrival of Islam.

Much later, when the pattern of the monsoon winds was understood in the Roman world, trade routes shifted from the land to the sea, and the interior of the Hadramaut became secluded, until Hadrami merchants from the hinterland developed new businesses, trading goods overseas as far as South East Asia from the eighteenth century onwards.

In more recent times, up until South Yemen gained its independence from the British in 1967, many urban areas of the Hadramaut were under the rule of tribal Sultans, notably that of Al-Qu'aiti. Thereafter it was part of the Peoples Democratic Republic of Yemen (PDRY), with its capital in Aden, until unification with the Yemen Arab Republic occurred in 1990.

To the east of Hadramaut is Mahrah province, a remote, sparsely populated agricultural region, rarely visited by travellers, which borders the Sultanate of Oman. Its principal town is the coastal settlement of Al-Ghaydah. In past times this region was famed for its sailors and the incense it produced. The language of the people here is Mahri, which, like the related languages of Dhofar, the Kuria Muria (or Halaaniyaat) Islands and Socotra has its roots in the ancient languages of south Arabia. There is no written version.

Away from the coast the centre of Arabia is a vast area of gravel plain partially covered in sand dunes. The main sand desert in the eastern part of the peninsula, the Rub al-Khali (the Empty Quarter), has a much smaller southern arm known as the Ramlat as-Sabatayn. It is 100km wide at its western end near the Yemen foothills, tapering to about 15km as it enters the Wadi Hadramaut. It consists of chains of dunes or *uruq* (*urq*) which are roughly parallel, with a general east-west orientation, separated by narrow flats of gravel, silt or gypsum locally called *shuquq* (*shuq*). Some of the dune ridges can be as much as 50m high and they are often several kilometres long. They do move, although the seasonal variation in wind direction generally nullifies any overall change. The east-west route from Marib to Shabwa, used by four-wheel drive vehicles to cross the northern side of the Ramlat as-Sabatayn, is one of the incense routes used by camel caravans in antiquity between Hadramaut, Marib and western Saudi Arabia. In places, outcrops of old metamorphosed Precambrian basement rocks, notably marble and quartzite, break through the sand-covering and along its eastern edge, scattered low hills and mesas of Cretaceous rocks, some capped by Palaeocene limestones (e.g. Jebel al-Abr), and salt domes of late Jurassic age such as Milh Kharwah and Iyad protrude

On the desert fringe, overlooking the entrance to the Wadi Hadramaut, a mesa, the Jebel al-Abr (*above*), dominates the scene. *Below*, a bedouin of the region strikes a sheikhly pose, wearing his ceremonial *jambia*.

Hadramaut's dunes, the Ramlat as-Sabatayn (*right*), comprise a south-western arm of the vast Rub al-Khali – the world's greatest sand desert stretching right across southern Arabia.

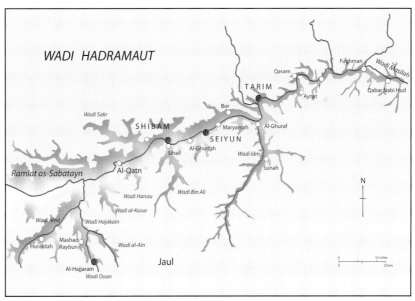

WADI HADRAMAUT

Wadi Sakr

SHIBAM

SEIYUN

Sihail

Al-Ghurfah

TARIM

Bor

Maryamah

Al-Ghuraf

Qasam

Aynat

Fughman

Wadi Masilah

Qabar Nabi Hud

Al-Qatn

Ramlat as-Sabatayn

Wadi Hanau

Wadi al-Kasar

Wadi Bin Ali

Wadi Idm

Sunah

Wadi Amd

Wadi Hajakain

Wadi al-Ain

Huraidah

Mashad
Raybun

Al-Hajjarain

Wadi Doan

Jaul

N

0   10 miles
0   20 km

through the veneer of sand. Around its margins, many wadi courses extend for several kilometres into the Ramlat before disappearing under the sand.

The ancient dam at Marib is one of the wonders of prehistory.

Interdunal lakes once formed at the end of wadis flowing into the centre of the desert. This has given rise to the strange phenomenon, visible when crossing the desert, of what appears to be seashells in the desert sand. They are not in fact seashells but part of a Quaternary molluscan fauna which once inhabited the area. They are a combination of terrestrial and aquatic snail shells (gastropods). *Melanoides tuberculata*, the most prolific lacustrine form, is recognised by its slender shape and delicate beaded surface sculpture. They seem somewhat out of place considering today's dry climate, and are actually very recent fossils, from a time when the climate was much kinder. The internal desert lakes dried up eventually with the onset of the present climatic regime between 4000 and 3000 BC, leaving their unfortunate residents somewhat high and dry.

Marib

In ancient times Marib, 120km from Sana'a in the Wadi Adhana region, was a major centre of the Sabaean empire, the oldest, most celebrated and powerful of the south Arabian kingdoms. Ultimately it became the capital of the kingdom, supplanting Sirwah, 35km to the west. Today, the old mud town of Marib is in ruins. The discovery of oil 100km to the east in the Jauf al-Batin

Marib, close upon three millennia ago, rose to become the economic and cultural centre of the Sabaean empire. It survived until late in the first millennium AD. The southern sluice of the old Marib Dam is shown above.

area has led to the development of a new town nearby. Old Marib, on the north side of the Wadi as-Sadd, now has few inhabitants (it was badly bombed in the 1962-8 civil war). Many believe that this is the site of Bilqis' the Queen of Shebas' palace of Salhin, said by tradition to have been built by djinns. Nearby, the old mosque's ceiling is held up by Sabaean pillars.

In 1951, the American archaeologist Wendell Phillips obtained permission from Imam Ahmad to excavate at Marib. The team, led by Frank Albright, spent about nine months in the area during 1951-2, and worked under a tremendous amount of local pressure and suspicion – especially when squeezes (a type of rubbing) of Sabaean inscriptions were made. Eventually they had to leave, rushing over the border to Bayhan in the West Aden Protectorate leaving all their finds behind. Many can now be seen in the National Museum in Sana'a.

Marib Dam

Marib is also the site of one of the world's great ancient structures – a magnificent feat of early engineering and masonry techniques. This is the dam across Wadi Adhana, the largest wadi in the south Arabian highlands. Its purpose was to hold and to divert the water, which flooded down the wadi

from time to time during the rainy season, over the nearby agricultural land. It would have also allowed the water to soak into the ground and recharge the aquifers, thus supplying the wells. Recent excavations by the German Archaeological Institute show that, while the structure whose impressive remains standing here today was erected in the eighth century BC, irrigation works in the Wadi Adhana at Marib were undertaken at least from the beginning of the second millennium BC. The two masonry sluices of the much-repaired eighth-century dam remain: the northern one, usually approached

The stylae (top) carries the script of the prevailing south Arabian language of ancient times, Himyaritic. The great pillars, seen above, comprised the propylon of the temple of ancient Marib, capital of Saba (Sheba).

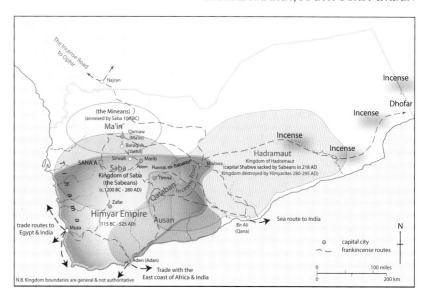

Map of the Ancient Kingdoms and Trade Routes.

first, and the southern one on the other side of the wadi, which is more extensive and almost as high as it was originally. They demonstrate the Sabaeans' skill in quarrying the stone blocks, cutting and dressing them, transporting them to the site and then erecting them and binding them together with lead and iron. Between them once stretched the dam, an earth bank 600m long and 16m high covering a foundation of loose, broken stones. A little of this rockfill barrage remains and all along its line the massive piles of silt deposited by the floods can be seen. The sluices and spillways are carefully keyed into the limestone bedrock on either side of the wadi and show a range of interesting construction techniques used to increase the structure's strength, as well as the use of bituminous mortar. This is thought to have come from shales in the salt dome at Safir some 75km to the north-east (Raikes, 1977) and is best seen in the rubble core of the northern sluice. All this effort and craftsmanship testify to the highly-organised society that must have existed here in ancient times, as well as to the need for sophisticated and efficient irrigation systems in southern Arabia.

The dam is believed to have held up to 150,000 cubic metres of water. The remains of the irrigation system and the system of canals around the dam can still be seen on the plain in front of it. The dam must have irrigated over 10,000 hectares. As a result, the oasis here would have been enormous in the world of two thousand years ago, supporting between 25,000 and 50,000 Sabaeans, and probably allowing them to sell supplies of food and water to the caravans.

The dam gave way on a number of occasions, mainly due to flood water overtopping the earth bank as the depth was reduced by silting. One of the last such events was in AD 542, during the reign of Abraha the Axumite, who is famous for attempting to repair it. The final mention of the dam, around AD 570, appears in the Qur'an. It is suggested that the dam's final abandonment was due to a weakening political situation. Maintaining and repairing the long bank between one flood season and the next would have involved a great many labourers and much animal transport; this in turn would have required strong central control of the society which the dam served. Perhaps this was no longer available in a disintegrating state.

In 1986 a new dam was opened nearby as a gift from the late Shaikh Zaid Bin Sultan al-Nahayan of the United Arab Emirates, who believed himself to be a descendant of the tribes that moved north and east after the collapse of the Sabaean kingdom. This dam, which collects water from the Al-Balak mountain range, is said to be able to hold 400 million cubic metres of water.

Temples

The great temple of Marib, the Awwam (sometimes called Mahram Bilqis) is dedicated to the moon god Almaqah. It was partly excavated by Wendell Phillips' expedition of 1951-2. A series of monolithic pillars, probably the propylaeum, mark the entrance to the temple, which may have been used as a sanctuary. The finest sculpture of the ancient Arabs, a figurative bronze of a Sabaean nobleman Ma'adi Karib (of probably the seventh or eighth century BC) was found here. It is now in the National Museum.

The Arsh Bilqis – the Throne of Bilqis – is the second most important temple in Marib. A line of five elegant symmetrical pillars, also known as the Almaqah or Moon Temple, was built towards the end of the eighth century BC. This has now been extensively excavated, uncovering a broad temple floor surrounded by steps and inscribed marble plinths. It has a pure abstraction and geometrisation that can be seen in Yemeni structures even today.

Baraqish

Is this not the most impressive archaeological site and best-preserved ancient walled town in Yemen? It once had more than fifty towers and two gates, and its walls reached up to 14m high. Lying in the wide Wadi Fardha, it was previously known as Yathil, the dominant town in the Minaean kingdom and an important centre for the incense trade. The Sabaeans had controlled this whole region but, by the end of the great Sabaean era in 410 BC, Main broke away and formed an alliance with Hadramaut to open up new caravan routes and thus increase trade. We know that the town had good connections with the Mediterranean. Inspired by tales of royal towns and palaces in Arabia, the Emperor Augustus instructed the proconsul of Egypt, Aelius Gallus, to invade the peninsula and seize the wealth of the citadels of which he had heard so much. In 24 BC a force of 10,000 Romans and 15,000 mercenaries was assembled and sent to the region with Nabataean guides. It captured and garrisoned Baraqish but failed to take Marib. The force never got back to the Mediterranean and the Romans never tried a land invasion again. They did come back by sea, however, once they had understood the pattern of the monsoons. In the main area of the site, the remains of a dome, a mosque, a well and tower stand amidst great sherds of pottery and glass. Elsewhere an Italian archaeological team has recently excavated a temple which still had its roof and contained stone tables equipped with bulls' heads at the end. These may have been for sacrifices; the temple is thought to be to a god of healing.

Shabwa

The salt mine at Shabwa (*above*) was the source of a major industry which played its part right up to recent times in Yemen's collective economy.

Shabwa is north of present day Ataq on the edge of the Ramlat as-Sabatayn. It stands on two hills near the town of Irma, the principal ruined city and religious centre of the ancient state of Hadramaut. Today, the remains of palaces, walls, streets and steps suggest a sophisticated past; a French archaeological team has been working there for many years. Shabwa has been identified with Sabota – the place Pliny described as having 60 temples, an important stopping-place on the incense road – although evidence of the early salt mines suggests this was a trading route long before the heyday of the incense trade. The buildings in the region are made of stone and lime, and much of the ruins have been reused for local building.

Other sites at Timna, by Bayhan, Raybun and Zafar and Qana at Bir Ali are all worth seeing, although little is known about their origins and development.

Salt deposits found in domes near Shabwa are still mined for local consumption using simple tools, much as they have been for centuries. The rock salt was formed about 150 million years ago but has only recently flowed to the surface due to the density difference between the salt and the overlying rocks. There are at least ten of these deposits in the vicinity of the Ramlat as-Sabatayn, and most of them were mined in antiquity; they include Shabwa, Safir, Bayhan, Iyadh (Haid al-Milh), Ayadim, Layadin (Jebel al-Milh), Al-an-Nuqub and Milh Kharwah. Their presence is thought to be the principal reason behind the siting of the ancient city of Shabwa, and even before then – in Neolithic times, when the climate was wetter – these deposits would anyway have influenced the movements of game and attracted Neolithic hunter populations to the region.

Inscriptions

South Arabian belongs to the southern Semitic group of languages – which includes Arabic, the Ethiopian Semitic languages and more recent and contemporary Southern Arabian languages – the remnants of which are still current in such Yemeni survivals as Mahri, Shuhuri and Socotri, which are spoken in Yemen and Oman. Little research has been done into the relationship between these and other ancient languages, but it is known that they have connections with modern Arabic and Geíz, the liturgical language of Ethiopia. Thousands of inscriptions in ancient South Arabian, made on stone or bronze, have been discovered, and many have now been interpreted. The texts tend to have religious significance or else document the history of a people, their leaders, events and the building of significant structures. They mention many gods, but there is no poetry nor literature, nor even numbers to be found.

The origins of the South Arabian alphabet are unknown. Some suggest that, like the Greek, Latin, Arabic and Hebrew alphabets, it has its roots in the Phoenician alphabet, which was made up of 29 consonants – vowels were not inscribed. What is perhaps most astonishing is its stability, for between its emergence in the sixth century BC and its disappearance in the seventh century AD only two rather infrequent letters changed shape. The ancient languages of the six major kingdoms of south Arabia were probably rather similar and, like Arabic, were read from right to left – although some inscriptions before 500 BC are written in boustrophedon (lines that read from right to left and left to right alternately). The earliest examples of Sabaean inscriptions are probably those found on smooth rocks throughout southern Arabia, some of the best being from around Marib, where ancient scripted lintels are also seen above doors. Other ancient inscriptions can be seen recycled in more recent buildings, such as the gateways of the highland towns of Amran and Thula.

Many copies and impressions of early inscriptions were collected by early travellers to Yemen. Joseph Arnaud, a French pharmacist working in the 1830s and 1840s was one of them; he visited the Sabaean centres of Marib and Sirwah in disguise accompanied by a bedouin guide, probably being the first European to see them since antiquity. His copies of 56 Sabaean inscriptions, along with those copied in 1834-5 by Lieutenant J R Wellstead at Husn al-Ghurab, the rocky outcrop of Bir Ali, and at Nakab al-Hajar some distance inland, eventually laid the foundations for interpretation of South Arabian Semitic script in 1841 by Emil Rodiger and Wilhelm Gesenius.

Anyone who takes the short cut from Marib into the Hadramaut across the Ramlat as-Sabatayn, can see the profusion of bedouin settlements, sustained through animal husbandry, so evident after the rains. Camels – essential to life in the desert, can be seen in abundance and provide not just transport but thirst-quenching milk, food and clothing. There are also goats, whose thicker milk is processed and dried. Today, the men are more likely to be seen in a four-wheel drive vehicle than riding their camels.

Details of the building of Shabwa show the precision of the stonework which has survived for centuries. *Below,* the same precision is evident in part of the wall of the Marib Dam, bearing a Sabaean inscription.

The hard woods – often imported from India or Africa – of the doors and lintels adorning the houses of Shibam are carved in intricate relief by master craftsmen. Here are four examples.

Shibam

The old walled city of Shibam is named after King Shibam bin Harith ibn Saba who ruled from here. It was a major city on the overland spice and incense route.

Although its origins are still not completely understood, it was trading at the time of the Sabaeans around the fourth and fifth centuries BC. The present settlement seems to have been established around the third century AD, after the destruction of Shabwa. In the seventh century AD the people of Shibam were converted to Islam, the first community on the Wadi Hadramaut to adopt the new religion. It has been the commercial and political capital of Hadramaut many times. More recently, it was the commercial capital of the Wadi Hadramaut until 1940, when an airport was built east of Seiyun, and the economic centre of gravity moved there.

Shibam is made up of domestic, commercial, educational, administrative and religious buildings – a small walled city that is a complete unit in itself. It has seven mosques, including the Rashid Mosque (sometimes called the Masjid al-Jum'a, the Friday mosque), which dates back to the early tenth century. Its unique architectural heritage of 500 mud-brick houses is an extraordinary example of traditional Yemeni building skills. Some of these houses are many centuries old and rise up to seven or eight storeys, the tallest reaching 30m. The city's towering appearance prompted Freya Stark to describe it as 'the Manhattan of the desert'. It results partly from the fact that it is built on a mound made up of the remains of earlier towns. The impression is enhanced by the abundance of windows, usually open, with wooden shutters, or harem grilles, and ventilation openings – often two at different levels on each floor; and by the long lines of shadows cast by the corners and edges of buildings in the afternoon sun. The city was added to UNESCO's World Heritage list in 1982.

Those who can afford it limewash their houses to protect them against termites and against the rains and flooding which occur from time to time in the *sa'il*, the bed of the main wadi. (Living in a fortress can have advantages in protecting the residents from the vagaries of nature as well as mankind; the worst floods to affect the city took place as long ago as 1298 and 1532, and more recently in 2008). In general, the windowless lower floors are used for grain storage, with areas for domestic use above and those for family and leisure above that. The main room on the second floor is used by men for socialising. It often has wonderful carved plasterwork and free-standing decorated wooden columns supporting the ceiling, while women's areas are found higher, usually on the third or fourth floor. The highest rooms are for communal use by the whole family, and on the upper levels there are often bridges (*mi'bar*) and doors connecting the houses. These are a defensive feature, but also a practical one – especially for old people who find it difficult to walk up and down the interminable staircases.

As in the highlands, the houses open onto communal streets – a typical Yemeni characteristic – and are built around one of Shibam's five main open squares, or *sahat*, where men are seen playing dominoes and children a variety of hopscotch. Few houses have courtyards, although the walled house is becoming more common as people are encouraged to build and own land in

new areas outside the city. The craftsmen who build these new houses mostly live in Sihail Shibam, across the road from the main city, which has become something of an overflow area.

A notable feature in the older part of Shibam is the ornamental woodwork of windows and doors. The geometrically carved *khalfah* window screens, that can usually be seen on the major frontages of buildings are diverse and visually stunning (some even show South-East Asian influences). They are often carved from the wood of the hardy *'ilb* tree, which grows locally and is a major source of wood for craftsmen and for building, although imported woods such as teak are now increasingly used. Felled in winter, when there is little sap in it, the *'ilb* wood is practically insect-proof and is seen as indestructible when used on the interior of the house, and very long-lasting when used on the outside. The detailed carving of the doors and shutters – some dating back 300 years – is one of Shibam's major features.

For much of the year, the wadi bottom (*sa'il*) running along the edge of the city of Shibam provides a playing field for the local young. But there will be times in the year when it will be a torrent of water.

The old walled city of Shibam, *below*, the 'Manhattan of the desert' is an extraordinary example of traditional Yemeni building skills and was added to UNESCO's World Heritage list in 1982. Grace, serenity, and intimacy characterise traditional living and traditional houses (*above* and *right*).

Above, birds spot the dawn sky across the Wadi Hadramaut.

The ibex has historically been of great symbolic importance to southern Arabians. It is their sacred animal. Ibex horns are frequently fixed to rooftops, where they are one of the commonest forms of decoration. The horns of an ibex placed over the entrance to a house or high up on the corner of a building is usually associated with a charm against the evil eye and to bring good luck.

Today, there are still dances in the interior of the Hadramaut at which the dancers hold ibex horns above their heads in a ceremonial re-enactment of a time when the ibex hunt was a commonplace event. Until quite recently the ibex hunt ceremony was part of an ancient ritual to invoke rain to water the crops.

While musicians celebrate a wedding in Husn Square (*top, right*) traditional life continues in Shibam in the tower houses (*above*) and arched entrance way.

Main doors commonly have an 'unlocking box' beside them on the outside. This carved aperture is just large enough to allow an arm through to unlock the door from the inside, using a traditional wooden pronged key; the heavy bolt can then be pushed back and the door opened. There is also access to the latch mechanism from the inside of the house by means of a cord running up through the building. This allows those on any floor to open the door and allow visitors in without the need to run downstairs.

There are still master builders living and working in Hadramaut, constructing towering buildings in a way that has been practised for centuries. Foundations of local stone and chippings are laid in a trench cut out of the dry earth, and, in many buildings, a strip of stone wall is then erected to support the walls above. These are built of mud brick – often using larger bricks for the ground floors and a smaller size for the upper floors. Bricks are laid down in a specific way, and the walls tapered so that they grow thinner as the house rises. Finishing involves the application of a smooth coating of earth or lime plaster for protection against weather and insects. A mud building of the Hadramaut is not erected in one continuous operation but in stages. Each stage, which takes a month or more to complete, depending on the thickness of walls and the weather conditions, is given time to dry out in the sun before the next is added.

The bricks are made on site from wet mud mixed with chaff or chopped straw. Traditionally, the mud was taken from around the roots of the palm trees, where there was a good amount of binding clay in the mixture; this practice has now been restricted and mud is taken from open land or else recycled from old buildings. The latter practice is not satisfactory, as the straw content weakens over time. The mixture is packed into simple frames and the bricks turned out and left to dry in the sun before stacking.

A few kilometres outside Seiyun, on the way to Tarim, the tomb of Ahmad bin 'Isa al-Muhajir stands by the roadside. This is a place of pilgrimage, the burial place of a reformer who arrived 1,200 years ago, re-establishing orthodox Islam and influencing the religious life of the area. The site has special significance for women, because a holy woman – a *shaikhah* – is also buried here. Seiyun is the largest town of the Wadi Hadramaut, and the provincial capital and main government, commercial and communications centre. It is known for the fabulous palm groves that surround it and for its old market (organised by guilds, like the one in Sana'a) where traditional crafts such as jewellery are still practised. The town, which has a history going back thousands of years, probably owes its origin to this market, once an important stopping-place on the early trade route that ran east through Wadi Masilah and on to Shihr on the coast. Over many years the gathering of people here led to an urban centre being developed with houses, mosques and schools.

In 1494 there was an influx of people of the Hamdani tribes from north of Sana'a. Their leader was Amir Badr ibn Tawariq Kathiri, the ancestor of the Kathiri Sultans who ruled from their capital here from 1516 until independence from the British in 1967. The massive Sultan's Palace, with its four corner towers, stands in the oldest part of Seiyun, next to the busy market; it is the largest mud-brick building in the Wadi Hadramaut and an outstanding example of mud architecture. It was built in 1873, rebuilt in 1926 by Mansur bin Ghalib al-Kathiri and whitewashed by his son Ali in 1935. Today, it houses a museum of archaeology with finds from Raybun, one of Yemen's most important ancient sites, as well as exhibits on popular traditions, folklore and costumes. It also includes objects from the colonial days.

Some 35km east of Seiyun, encircled by palm groves, is Tarim, which takes its name from a local king, Tarim ibn Hadramaut ibn Saba al-Assgar. This was a major centre for the Kathiri state until the 1960s; it was the capital of the Hadramaut in ancient times and has been the religious capital of the Wadi Hadramaut since the tenth century. Its history, like Shibam's, is related to the rise of the Himyar kingdom and the destruction of Shabwa. Along with Zabid in the Tihama, it is a centre of learning of the Shafi'i school of Sunni Islam,

As readers of the Bible know, bricks without straw do not survive – and straw to this day is the vital constituent of Hadramaut's brick-making industry. The goats (*opposite*) will no doubt attend to the tidying up.

partly due to descendants of the 'Alawi Sayyids, who claim descent from the Prophet. They came from Basra, in southern Iraq, in 931, and the tomb of the founder Sayyid Ahmad Ba'Isa al-'Alawi, at the foot of a cliff between Tarim and Seiyun, is still visited to this day.

Tarim's reputation as a centre of religious teaching extended well beyond the Arabian Peninsula, reaching East Africa and South East Asia. This led to a rapid expansion during the seventeenth to nineteenth centuries, with the building of Qur'anic schools and mosques teaching orthodox Sunni Islam. Locals will tell you that there was once a mosque for each day of the Islamic year. (This was mainly due to the building of mosques by returned merchants as a thanks offering for the wealth and business prosperity they had won in South East Asia.) One of the most impressive, with its South East Asian influences

The massive Sultan's Palace, complete with four tall corner towers, stands in the oldest part of Seiyun, and is an outstanding example of mud architecture (*above*).

Left, a lime-washed mud brick building in Wadi Doan.

Right, local contemporary embroidery as displayed in Seiyun museum.

and 50-metre-high minaret, is the Al-Muhdhar mosque. Built in 1915, it is one of the great symbols of Yemeni architecture. Tarim is also known for its libraries, the most famous being the Al-Kaf Manuscripts Library, which houses around 5,000 manuscripts from the surrounding region covering religion, the thoughts of the prophets, Islamic law, Sufism, medicine, astronomy, agriculture, biography, history and mathematics. Many go back hundreds of years, and often contain vibrantly-coloured illuminations and illustrations.

The architecture of Tarim is more varied than that of any other Hadramaut town. The town's building boom began in the nineteenth century and reached its height between the late 1920s and the early 1940s. Elements of a neo-classical style are detectable in many of the buildings. In particular, the great fantasy structures financed by the ruling and trading families – particularly the al-Kaf family – illustrate the exceptional skills of its master craftsmen and builders. Although the practical building methods are the same, Tarim's architectural medley is completely different in character from the architecture of other regions of the Hadramaut. The buildings are lower and wider than the skyscraper structures of Shibam or the fortress-like structures elsewhere in the region; coloured glass is inset into wooden screens for windows; cool-coloured limewash covers parts of the walls, and various styles shout at you from all corners of the town. Moghul line and decoration from India or South East Asia (Singapore, Java and Malaysia) mingle with western neoclassical and baroque and even the beginnings of an art deco style on both the exteriors and interiors of buildings. The all-pervading mixture of influences – and the money for the building programmes – stemmed from businessmen and sailors

At Seiyun, the architectural jewel is the Sultan's Palace, seen on these pages in its frontal beauty and in details of windows, towers and appliqué flag, as well as views from high windows.

The tomb of Ahmad bin 'Isa al-Muhajir is today a place of pilgrimage on the roadside a few kilometres on the road to Tarim — commemorating the zeal of the reformer of twelve hundred years ago. A holy shaikhah is also buried there, honouring the sanctity of women.

In Tarim, the motorised gadgets of the west supplement rather than supplant the eastern way of life.

returning to their native town after years of trading with India and South East Asia.

Some 65km west of Shibam, near where the main road turns south, is the Wadi Doan, the main historic overland route between Mukalla on the coast and the Wadi Hadramaut. Near its mouth are the small settlement of Mashhad Ali and the white beehive mausoleum of Ali Hassan al-Attas (d. 1172), a religious leader known for his diplomatic skills. If you continue southwards up the wadi, you come to Al-Hajjarain, which, unusually for the Hadramaut, is built on a rock outcrop rather than along the wadi rim (siting buildings away from the most fertile land in the wadi has always been a top priority here). It is a pre-Islamic site and has a cistern dating from the Himyarite period. The bluffs above the wadi are of rock from the Eocene era; many of the houses clinging to them date back over four hundred years. This is believed to be the site of the first human settlement in Hadramaut. The Yemeni geographer Muhammad al-Hassan Hamdani described it as an extremely prosperous city in the tenth century; it is still a major town.

The South Coast

Across the Jaul to the south of the Wadi Hadramaut lie the Gulf of Aden and its two main historic ports of Mukalla and Shihr. In his *Travels* Marco Polo wrote of Shihr in the thirteenth century as one of the most barren places in the world. He described it as a huge city with a good harbour, where heavily laden ships from India docked. It was renowned for the quality of its incense, and ships from here carried vast numbers of Arabian chargers and saddle horses to India, where, we are told, they were sold to the king and his brothers – although no specific ruler's name is mentioned – at a great profit. Arabian merchants from Shihr, Aden, Dhofar and Hormuz all participated in this trade and sold thousands of horses every year. But by the year end only about a hundred or so were left, as no farriers lived in India and none were allowed to go there so that the export trade would continue year-on-year.

Hans Helfritz wrote in the 1930s of 'Mukalla, a city of glistening whiteness, of extraordinary beauty, with its countless palaces and lofty towers, lies in a

The Palace of the Dome, Qasr al-Qubbah (*opposite*) stands in the western part of Tarim, in an orchard garden. Once the house of Mohammed bin Husayn al-Kaf, it is now a hotel. The Al-Muhdhar Mosque (*right*) is known for the height and Moghul elegance of its minaret.

The Munaysurah Mansion of Tarim (*left*) bespeaks wealth and power.

Tarim is honoured for its libraries, of which the most celebrated is the Al-Kaf Manuscripts Library. Ali Salem Bukair (*pictured left*) is its librarian and manuscript artist.

delightful bay close under the dark cliffs of the Jebel el Kara. It is the gateway to the province of Hadramaut.' Crammed between one of Yemen's great volcanic mountain regions and the sea, it is approached either by the coast road from Aden or from Seiyun in the Wadi Hadramaut. This road passes through a succession of wadis and interesting towns and crosses the Jaul, a semi-desert mountain plateau. In the past, most non-Hadramis would have approached it by sea.

Al Qu'aiti borders were marked by customs posts – like the fort of Husn al-Mutahar (*right*) on the road to Tarim.

Overleaf, shepherdesses herd their goats near Wadi Doan.

Above is seen the face of the Ishshah Palace in Tarim, the house of 'Umar bin Shaykh al-Kaf. The pillars of the earth-built Munaysurah Mansion, Tarim, *above right,* have a Hellenistic confidence to them.

Mukalla has been of great importance for many centuries, with its trade extending to India and South East Asia as the many Indian influences in its architecture show. Locals will tell you that the town was founded in 1625 by a Yafa'i sultan, Ahmad bin Madyam al-Kasadi. In 1914 it took over from Shihr, some 50km to the east, as capital of the Hadramaut when the Qu'aitis (originally a tribe of the Yafa') transferred their capital. Now, as Yemen's third most important port (after Hodeidah and Aden), it is a centre for fishing and

Overleaf, the dramatic vista of Al-Hajjarain in Wadi Doan. Dense palm groves line the wadi, the proud buildings rising beyond.

Unmistakeably Yemeni, the gateway (*left*) gives on to the Qubbah Palace gardens.

Below, a woman on a donkey returns home to Al-Qatn.

Opposite, a street scene in today's Tarim. The great families took to classical forms for the splendour of their buildings, as evidenced by the capitals of the columns.

commerce along the country's vast south coast, and waterfront activities are still paramount. The town is roughly divided into two areas, the old town around the coastline, and the new town to the east, along the road to Riyan. In the busy modern harbour, traditional fishing boats bob at anchor in the swell; the waterfront along the coast from the old town is lined with white houses. Traders and businessmen from all over the Hadramaut congregate here, sitting in the alleyways and tea houses, and the busy lively centre of the main square is full of cafes bustling with workers and fishermen playing cards and dominoes. Everywhere in the narrow streets, Indian influence is betrayed by the design and carving of the beautiful old doors.

The town's architecture makes considerable creative use of gypsum and, in general, is distinctive for its South East Asian overtones and Indian inspiration, the latter evident everywhere in the narrow back streets where intricately carved doors and magnificent window screens can be found. The nightly illuminated ar-Rawdha and 'Umar mosques are delightful. (The traveller Jorgen Bisch writes in his book *Behind the Veil of Arabia* that the doors are so important around Mukalla that at times the door is erected first, and the house is then built around it.) The Sultan's Palace, which sits on the edge of the beach next to the town, was built in the late 1920s by Sultan 'Umar bin Awadh al-Qu'aiti and draws on the Indian and neoclassical styles.

From Mukalla the main road to Aden runs along the coast for 140km to Bir Ali, famous for its sandy beaches and craggy black basaltic lava fields dotted with small extinct volcanoes. One of these, the Husn al-Ghurab ('Crows' Fortress'), called Urr Mawiyat in ancient times, guards the entrance to a shallow harbour suitable only for small vessels.

Opposite, goats slake their thirst at a municipal watering trough in the Hadramaut.

The building techniques of Al-Hajjarain (*below*) have changed little down the centuries.

On its landward side, at the foot of the volcano, basalt blocks mark all that remains of the streets and houses of the ancient port of Qana (most of which has been cannibalised to provide building material for modern Bir Ali on the other side of the bay). There are references to it as Canneh in the Bible in the Book of Ezekiel, (27:23), written in about 600 BC, and in the works of Pliny

The Wadi Doan (*illustrated above and opposite*) is the principal historic route between Mukalla and the Wadi Hadramaut. At the Wadi's settlement of Sif a house rises in elegant colours (*above left*). Time and change have dealt less kindly with this settlement near Seiyun (*left*).

The men pictured here exhibit the
wide range of traditional headress –
from Marib province (*above left*)
to the Ras Hawra region, in
Hadramaut, (*top* and *above*).

Left, a Tarim shopkeeper awaits custom.

A Hadrami woman attends her family plantation of root crops.

Hadramaut Honey

Hadramaut honey, known for its rich, strong flavour, is famous throughout Arabia and is claimed to be the best (and is certainly the most expensive) honey in the world. It is used medicinally, as well as for food.

Beekeeping is probably one of the oldest forms of food gathering in the region, as evidenced by rock engravings in the area, and at one time practically every house in Wadi Doan had a beehive (many villages still have at least one beekeeper). There are various types of hive, including bored-out logs with removable wooden ends. These are usually made from the sukam (*Cordia abyssinica*), a broadleaved evergreen tree which grows around the edges of fields along the wadi floors (and is also used as a shade tree in highland coffee plantations).

There are two honey crops a year – November to March and June to August – with the honey harvested on the comb to ensure purity. The climate and the type of flora are crucial to the quality of the honey. Many beekeepers are nomadic, moving into areas where there are flowers for the bees to live off. The highest-quality honey comes from bees fed on natural flora such as desert bushes and the blossom of the 'ilb and sibr trees, rather than in cultivated vegetation areas.

composed in the first century AD. Qana's harbour and its position at the start of one of the overland trade routes for incense, myrrh and spices made it the main port of the kingdom of Hadramaut. Frankincense from Dhofar and Somalia and precious goods from India and Africa would have been unloaded from ships in the harbour into small boats and rafts and brought ashore to the waiting camel caravans. The Sabaeans became excellent seamen, sailing to Oman and Persia and also using the seasonal monsoon winds to take their ships to India, then bringing them back later in the year with silks, spices and fine cloth. In the second century AD, however, Qana was sacked (and possibly burned) by invaders, and from the end of the third century AD it slowly collapsed. In its heyday, the Husn al-Ghurab at Qana, which was reached from the town by a zigzag path, was topped with buildings, a watchtower and plastered masonry water tanks. The present crater is water-filled and connected to the open sea (as a result of undercutting by surf), while the flanks are coated

Husn Al-Ghuazi, (*above*) the over-hanging fortress, stands on the road from Riyan to Mukalla. It was built after the battle of Al-Bakarriya, and was once used as a customs post and guard house.

The city port of Shihr was one of the great centres of eastern commerce in the Middle Ages, when Marco Polo described it as being 'one of the most barren places in the world'. Through it were exported Arabian horses and incense, bringing wealth back to south Yemen. It remains a textile centre – as illustrated by the *futa* design (*right*).

The menfolk of Shihr (*above*) celebrate a wedding by dancing the *shabwani*. Lines two or three deep act out a battle, waving sticks and stamping.

Right, traditional weaving, Shihr.

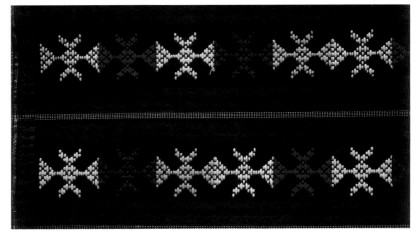

Up to the second century AD, the inlet of Bir Ali (or Qana as it was then known) was the main port of the kingdom of Hadramaut. An entrepôt for incense, it was mentioned by the Roman writer Pliny and the ancient Jewish text of Ezekiel also refers to it. It is seen (*left*) as it is today, where lines of ghost crab mounds dot the beach.

Left, the Wadi Hajar, Yemen's only perennial river.

in loose ash containing ejecta from the eruption, including some fine examples of spindle-shaped volcanic bombs (which form when the ejected lava spins through the air).

On the spit connecting Husn al-Ghurab to the mainland, and on quiet beaches all along the coast, sea turtles come ashore to lay their eggs. Burrowing ghost crabs, *Ocypode sp.*, also leave their mark in the form of regimented lines of mounds strung out along the strand line as on Bir Ali beach. These mounds

South Yemeni tradition has it that one of the Wise Men who attended Jesus Christ in Bethlehem soon after his birth came from Azzan (*opposite*).

built by the male ghost crabs are spaced with almost mathematical precision
on or above high tide mark. The males stand on the mounds to make a display,
which attracts females. By contrast, the females simply dig their burrows at
forty-five degrees into the shore, scattering the sand over the beach. They
emerge to feed on insects, sea turtle eggs and hatchlings, which are abundant
along these shores. The crabs actually run an efficient mining operation
probing and excavating the beach for its treasure of turtle eggs. Although they

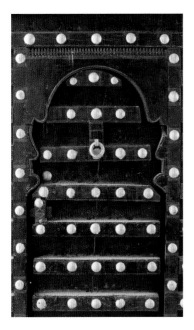

The view of the city's waterfront, showing Al-Shahid stretching out into the bay of Khalf, shows part of the natural haven the port comprises. It was founded in 1625 by Ahmed bin Madyem al-Kesadi, a Yafa'i Sultan. Its architecture shows distinct Indian and South East Asian influences. Its rolling hinterland can be seen opposite.

are always on the lookout, their daytime sorties indicate that the threat to their lives from predators is not extreme. The greatest potential danger to them would come from black kites, but these are generally absent along the coast between Aden and Oman. In their efforts to escape back to the burrow they are able to run forwards, backwards or sideways across the sand at speeds of up to 16 kilometres an hour. It is hardly surprising the family name *Ocypodidae* in Greek means 'swift-footed'.

The houses (*left*) in the Hadrami region of Ataq show the characteristic colouring of the local clay, and the regional style of crenellation.

Pictured below is a detail of a house in Lawdar, through which the traveller passes on his way via Al-Bayda to Dhamar.

West of Bir Ali, the main road continues along the coast for a while but then turns north and climbs inland. Eventually it reaches Habban, a magnificent town on the edge of the Wadi Habban, with its massive clay housing complexes, traditional mosques and clumps of acacias and fruit trees. The town is home to a religious aristocracy and was well known for the work of some of its population of 300 Jewish silversmiths, in its day the best in southern Yemen. Habban was severely affected when Yemeni Jews left for Israel after 1948; the craft is now lost and today many of its houses are deserted.

Nearby, the major town of the Shabwah Governate, Ataq, lies on a broad sandy plain flanked on the west by hills of granite, to the east by a sandstone escarpment and to the north by three low volcanic hills of very recent origin. The main road runs through Al-Mahfid where traditional mud buildings have taken on a new elegance with brightly coloured windows and shutters. Further westwards along the uplands towards Lawdar there are some interesting buildings on which external decoration using stone set into cement has produced a creative and contemporary vernacular style. From Lawdar one road leads up the magnificent Kaur al-Audhillah escarpment, which offers some outstanding views down to the Gulf of Aden. It passes through Al-Bayda and Rada to Dhamar where it joins the main route from Taiz to Sana'a.

On the edge of the Wadi Habban, (*above right*) stands the striking city of the same name, with its massive clay housing complexes and mosques. It is well known for its silver and was once home to a population of 300 Jewish silversmiths, whose departure for Israel in 1948 have left it deprived.

The face of the old and the new are evident in the buildings pictured *above*, Azan (*top*) and Ataq (*above*).

South and east of here stretches the discontinuous coastal Lawdar Plain, which is of variable width and is bordered by a coastal mountain belt. The plain itself is composed largely of gravel flats and alluvium interrupted by cliffs of older rock and some tracts of recent lavas, as well as Pliocene and recent raised beaches, terraces and dune areas. Many of the wadis fade out in sand dunes within a couple of kilometres or so of the sea, although a flow of water continues underground in channels which can be roughly traced from the alignments of trees and shrubs.

North-east of the coastal town of Shuqrah, 120km east of Aden, the main road passes through a vast volcanic field covering an area of 4,000sq km. Volcanic rocks here consist of black alkali basalt flows, which have filled irregularities in the pre-existing landscape. These flowed from the conspicuous maroon coloured cinder cones dotted around the area, notably the larger ones of Hamisha and Mirkibu. The flows are so recent and their preservation so good that when you enter this landscape you would be excused for thinking that the eruptions had just taken place. It is possible to see the flow fronts and the rubbly surface layer of solidified lava blocks, which were carried on the top of the moving lava as on a conveyor belt. Lavas generally flowed southwards towards the sea and have formed a gently sloping lava plain 100m thick in places with individual flows travelling up to 10km.

The cinder cones are perfectly preserved heaps of loosely packed basaltic scoria and thin lava flows. Steam percolating through them has oxidised the iron in the rock to an attractive deep reddish-brown colour which makes them easy to spot in the landscape. Similar features can also be seen in the newest Miocene-Pliocene volcanic centres of Amran, Marib, and Dhamar further north.

These volcanoes represent a single eruptive episode which lasted between a few hours and a few years; once an eruption ceased the source of the magma

The edge of the Shuqrah volcanic field. This has been extensively described by Cox et al. (1977). A barren unforgiving landscape of recent lava flows with rubbly surface layers which have flowed from the cinder cones in the far distance.

Below, a section through the progressive eruption sequence in the Shuqrah volcanic field showing thin layers of airborne ash, followed by loosely packed lumps of reddish scoria, a frothy basaltic ash ejected from the vent, and later basalt lava flows.

froze over and the volcano never erupted again. Volcanic activity probably lasted a few thousand years in total. Each layer deposited around the cone is a result of successive pulses of eruption. Together they tell the story of the course of the eruption itself. Construction of the road passing through this area has exposed the flanks of some of these cones, and it is possible to see the regular sequence of sloping layers which make them up. A range of different rock types, each representing a different part of the eruption, can be distinguished. The black spongy rock with large elongated bubbles is a vesicular basalt which formed within the main mass of the solid lava as dissolved water and carbon dioxide tried to escape when the magma depressurised on eruption. The material with a pleated surface caused by chilling of the moving lava skin is ropey basalt. There is also reddish scoria, a light frothy basaltic ash which was ejected from the volcano and built up around the vent to form the cone. Today the active volcanic centres in the area are restricted to a few in Saudi Arabia along the Red Sea, Ethiopia and, most recently, Jebel al-Tair in the Red Sea, which erupted in 2007.

Further west along the coast, Zinjibar sits in the coastal delta of the Wadi Bana, known for its fertility and agriculture, and sometimes for disputes about precious water resources between the tribes of Fadhli and Lower Yafa'. Finally, the road arrives in the Crater district of Aden. Here, just before the land runs out, it is joined by the road that runs down the Wadi Tiban from the north, linking the city with the highlands and the Tihama.

Aden

Unlike many of the towns of Yemen, Aden, the country's second city, is largely composed of buildings in a modern style that tells of its colonial past,

The spiny tailed lizard, or dhab, like the one seen here in Shuqrah (right), are found in rocky areas. They survive the dry climate by absorbing almost all the water they need from the plants they eat.

and asserts the city's importance as an international port for much of the nineteenth and twentieth centuries. Aden was only a small fishing village with about five hundred inhabitants when the British first secured the area in 1839. But it possesses one of the world's best-sheltered natural deep-water harbours. This, with its position near the entrance to the Red Sea, made it an ideal base from which to dominate maritime traffic eastwards from Egypt and to protect regional trade. It also served as a coaling station, and, after the opening of the Suez Canal in 1869, its bunkering role became greatly significant. In the twentieth century the construction of an oil refinery and improved bunkering facilities ensured that in 1957 Aden, by now a free port, was handling so much shipping that it ranked third in the world after London and New York; in fact, it developed into a sort of colonial city-state. From 1967 to 1990 it was capital of independent South Yemen. More recently it has been designated the 'economic capital' of unified Yemen. In 1991 it was declared a 'free trade zone'.

However, use of Aden's excellent harbour and strategic location is not a modern phenomenon. Aden was crucial to ancient traders exploiting the seasonal monsoons to ply between India and the Mediterranean. As W B Harris wrote in 1893, 'Aden perhaps can claim an antiquity and an importance throughout all history, unparalleled for its size and its situation in the annals of the world. When countries, now the centres of vast civilisations, consisted of primeval forests, inhabited by almost primeval man, and filled with wild beasts, Aden was an emporium of trade. With every possible disadvantage except its harbour and its situation, it was inhabited by merchants, who collected and re-shipped by vessel and by caravan the wealth of many lands.'

In fact, Aden has a history recorded in writings and inscriptions going back at least 3,000 years to the kingdom of Ausan, which had a harbour here and traded extensively with the East African coastline. By 410 BC Aden was

Termites

Above, termite mound.

The panoramic verdancy (*opposite*) is of the Lawdar plain. It is a source of dependable crops – and has been husbanded for centuries.

Below, village near Al-Bayda

On the upper part of the south Arabian coastal plain tower-like termite mounds form a conspicuous feature of the landscape. They are irregular to conical in shape, rising to head height, and stand 50-100m apart along the wadi courses in Abyan province. Their builders are large colonies of the fungus-growing higher termite Macrotermes, most probably *Macrotermes subhyalinus*, a common sight in tropical Africa, where the genus originates, but fairly rare in the Arabian Peninsula where they occur sporadically here and in nearby Dhofar (Oman) and Saudi Arabia.

Not surprisingly, it takes a vast number of the tiny termites to produce such prodigious earthworks, and the termite colonies contain millions of individuals, some of them quite long-lived, each performing a different role in a highly organised colonial structure. The mounds, built up of a mixture of earth, saliva and clay that sets extremely hard, have a complex internal structure and ventilation system. A central chamber is inhabited by the king and queen termite, and a series of chambers of varying size and shape contain fungus combs which help the insects to break down the life-giving cellulose they harvest on the surface at night. *M. subhyalinus* feeds mainly on grass litter; this is stored in special chambers in the nest where it is allowed to ferment before it is eaten and deposited on the combs. After a few weeks the combs are broken down and the nutrients harvested.

The termites enter and leave the mound through a series of underground passageways, or foraging galleries, in its base, which radiate out under the surrounding area and come to the surface some distance away. Foraging takes place on the surface at night, and only during the day if food is in short supply.

The termites have become adapted to life in this semi-arid environment, and by means of some specially arranged hairs can extract water from the pores in the soil through capillary action. In general, they are largely inconspicuous except for annual migration flights – the means by which the colonies are able to spread. A proportion of winged migrating forms leave from temporary exit holes near the top of the mound. They are incapable of powerful flight and usually travel less than 100m. On landing, the males and females snap off their wings, find a partner and dig a tunnel to start a new colony as the new king and egg-producing queen. The first eight months in a new colony's life are a particularly vulnerable time for the queen, who loses about thirty per cent of her initial weight. Mortality rates at this stage are typically about fifty per cent.

Termites are, in a sense, the tropical equivalent of the temperate earthworm, helping to fertilise and enrich the soil, and are therefore especially important in dry climates, where ordinary decay is rather slow. One species however – *Microtermes najdensis*, which lives in the soil – is a particular pest in the cultivated wadi areas of the Tihama, causing substantial root damage to a wide range of crops, including cotton and maize.

North of Aden lies Lahej where camels (*left*) are in daily use. A mosque in Lahej (*right*) calls the faithful to prayer five times daily – but the local people follow the Qur'anic injunction of daily prayer wherever they may be, as in Wadi Tiban (*below*).

prospering under the Sabaeans; in 24 BC the Romans managed to capture it; and then for five hundred years, under the powerful Himyarites, it was an important transhipment centre for goods coming from India for onward transport to other Red Sea ports. For a while, it fell under Persian control, but by the sixth century, it was back in the hands of the Yemenis, although a preference for overland trade meant a decline in its importance for a time. Nonetheless, we know that Chinese silks had been coming to the Middle East from well before the advent of Islam, and some descriptions say that the sea routes via Yemen were preferred to those overland. Aden came under the control of the Sulaihi kingdom in the eleventh century, and when Queen Arwa of Jiblah came to the throne in the 1080s, she was said to receive an annual revenue of some 100,000 dinars from the port – an indication of the wealth of Aden even then.

Private documents and letters dating from the twelfth century, found in a synagogue in Cairo, mention Jewish merchants of this period who were based in or travelled through Aden, shipping goods from India on to Cairo and vice versa; copper, brass, lead and even recycled materials are mentioned, along with cloves, peppers, raisins and waxes. In the thirteenth century Marco Polo mentioned the city in his *Travels*, and in the fourteenth century Al-ʿUmari wrote that 'the bulk of [Aden's] wealth comes from the wares of merchants from India, Egypt and Abyssinia.' But by the 1500s Vasco da Gama's discovery of an alternative sea route via the Cape of Good Hope must have creamed off a good deal of the trade between Europe and India. Even so, Aden's wealth and strategic importance led the Portuguese Viceroy of the Indies, Alphonso d'Albuquerque, to take Socotra and use it as a base for an unsuccessful siege of the walled city in 1513. However, by 1538 (the year that the Ottomans occupied Yemen for the first time) it had fallen into the hands of Pasha Al-Khadim, Commander of Sulaiman the Magnificent's fleet.

In 1503, the Italian Ludovico di Varthema wrote: 'Aden is such mighty and powerful that I have hardly seen another city of its might during my lifetime – all big ships anchor at the port, coming from India, Ethiopia or Persia.' Certainly, this was no small fishing port – the city's population in the sixteenth century is believed to have been around 60,000. Nonetheless, during the seventeenth and eighteenth centuries the Portuguese, Turkish and Egyptian interest in Yemen rested on the coffee trade, which was based at Mukha and Hodeidah, not Aden.

In the 1730s the Sultan of Lahej, a member of the Abdali tribe, rebelled against the north, and trade interests naturally moved to Mukha, as centre of Yemen's coffee exports. Aden's prosperity was only restored after British interest led to it becoming a British territory in 1839 and the Suez Canal was built in 1869. The British had had their eye on the coffee trade monopolised by the Ottomans, and were concerned about Egyptian movements in the area, and also about American, French and Dutch vessels trading there. The East India Company vessel *Ascension* had visited Aden as early as 1609.

When Napoleon turned towards Egypt in 1798, the British captured the island of Perim to interdict the route to India. But it had to be abandoned for

Steamer Point in Aden has been the first landfall in south Arabia
for countless vessels for over a century and a half.

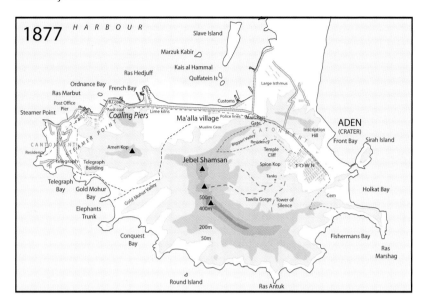

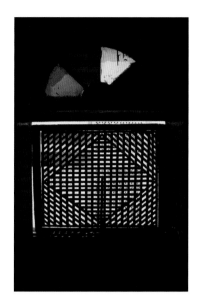

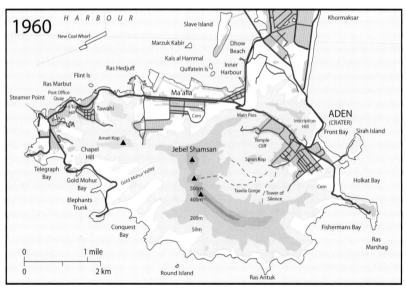

lack of water and the force took refuge in Aden where it was well received. Aden was then selected as a base to protect British trade interests in the southern Red Sea and as a coaling station, conveniently midway between Port Said and Bombay. A flotilla visited in 1829 with this in mind and in 1838 a decision was made to send Captain Haines from India both to obtain redress for the despoiling of a wrecked British vessel and to pursue the wider plan. He reached an agreement with the Sultan of Lahej for the cession of the territory against an annual pension. But when the Sultan failed to honour it, he took the place by assault. The Sultan made several attempts to retake Aden by force while the second son to succeed him tried to undermine the British position by turning the surrounding tribes against them. None of these ploys worked,

In the Crater region, a seller of dried Adeni peppers (*above*) works at his stall.

Top right, looking out from Goldmohur Beach, fishing nets are spread out across the bay of Aden.

and it stayed under the control of the British colonial administration in India until 1 April 1937, when it became a Crown Colony.

Most trade at the time was conducted on the other side of the water at Berbera in the Horn of Africa, where a great fair was held annually, and merchants from India, Arabia and Somalia gathered. Nomadic tribes in the vicinity refused to allow permanent buildings to be erected, however, so the Indian merchants, who knew the British well, saw Aden as the best place for conducting trade. Soon Somalis followed, crossing over to Aden and taking the African trade with them. At the same time, the coffee trade was diminishing as the Imam in north Yemen had a number of disputes with the ruler of Abu Arish and the Tihama, Sharif Hussain. By 1848 the Imam had control of Mukha and the trade virtually came to a halt. As a result, those trading in coffee came to British controlled Aden.

In 1853 Aden was declared a free port, and business immediately boomed. Most of the trading houses set up were Indian and Persian. Captain Luke Thomas founded an agency running commercial operations by sea, the first Briton to do so. Mail ships, taken over eventually by P&O, had a priority in the harbour, and steamship lines of many nations established depots at Hadjuf. By the 1850s and 1860s coal was offloaded from ships offshore by large numbers of workers, many of whom had come from the highlands of north Yemen or Mukha. Connections were developed with Zanzibar, where the trading agencies of many nations were based, and with similar centres.

At this time, the Crater area of Aden developed, Front Bay being the first landing place; warehouses and a customs house were built near Sirah Island.

Later, Ras Shaikh Ahmad and Ma'alla, where a pier was later built, became landing places. The entrance to Main Pass became a customs post. Permanent housing was developed, and Yemeni coffee houses filled with people trying to find employment, taking their leisure and collecting wages. With the opening of the Suez Canal in 1869, Yemenis were able to work and settle in ports further afield, among them Cardiff in the United Kingdom, once the largest coal-exporting port in the world. Steamships began to arrive in large numbers as the port developed, and by the end of the century, it could handle the largest ships of the day. The arrival of the telegraph in Aden in 1879 gave it an advantage over other Red Sea ports in the conduct of international trade.

Aden's air and naval bases played an important part in the second world war. Thereafter, it became the world's premier ship-bunkering port. Its oil refinery began operations in 1954, and soon trade flourished again; cargo was off-loaded, and goods en route from Europe to the Far East were transhipped and stored. Land was reclaimed on the seaward side of Ma'alla during the 1950s to build the Home Trade Quay for developing cargo operations. Passenger vessels called in, including cruise liners and ships taking emigrants to the southern hemisphere, and, as Aden was a free port, many passengers disembarked here for a few hours' duty-free shopping. As a result, the port had shops open for 24 hours a day.

The British left Aden in 1967 and the Colony, together with the East and West Aden Protectorates, Kamaran (later ceded to the YAR) and Perim, became an independent state as the People's Democratic Republic of Yemen. In the same year, the Suez Canal was closed as a result of the Arab-Israeli Six Day War (it was not reopened until 1975), and ships travelling to the Gulf, India and the Far East were therefore routed around the Cape of Good Hope. International traffic through the port of Aden plummeted. Moreover, the region was devastated by tyrannical Marxist methods of government and periodic political instability. The unification of North and South Yemen in 1990 greatly reduced both oppression and instability. Recent investment funnelled into the city in the form of a multi-purpose container terminal has enabled larger ships to berth and off-load foodstuffs and other cargoes. As a consequence Aden's fortunes as a major port have begun to revive.

Aden's cosmopolitan heritage assures its Roman Catholic visitors and residents their own church – which is overlooked by a mid-nineteenth-century colonial clocktower named 'Little Ben' after its loftier contemporary atop St Stephen's Tower of London's Houses of Parliament.

The Aden volcano and crater

The Aden peninsula is an extinct volcanic complex some six kilometres out to sea from the mainland to which it is joined by a narrow isthmus. A portion of the complex on the east of the peninsula is separated by open sea to form Sirah Island, and it is the protection given to Front Bay by this island which made this the bay to be selected as the original harbour of Aden. The low-lying land here is where the ancient town of Aden was first built. The main harbour of the modern era lies on the other side – the west – of the isthmus: a magnificent natural haven.

The crescent-shaped jagged range of Jebel Shamsan ('the mountain of two suns'), which dominates the Aden peninsula on the north, divides to give

A fruit bar provides shade and juicy refreshment in the midday heat.

access to the district known as Crater and the Tawila wadi in which the water storage tanks are built. The bulk of the city on the peninsula itself lies on a vast volcanic pile up to 550m thick covering an area of 30sq.km.

The volcano erupted massively between five and six million years ago, and raged over a period of one to one and a half million years, before becoming extinct, during which time the caldera which forms the present day Crater was formed. The volcanic site at Aden and those at Ras Imran, Little Aden and Bir Ali belong to a string of coastal volcanoes dotted along the southern margin of the Arabian plate.

Aden's waterside Ma'alla district has recently developed from its earlier role of bringing ashore barges of coal and other goods to being a multi-purpose container terminal for the entire country.

Left, at twilight across Aden harbour are visible the islands of Qulfatein, Kais al-Hammal and Marzuk Kabir.

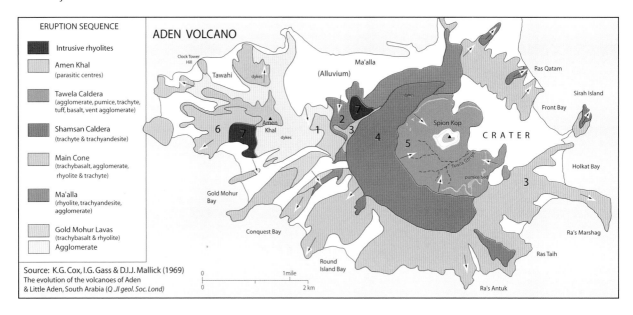

ERUPTION SEQUENCE

Intrusive rhyolites

Amen Khal
(parasitic centres)

Tawela Caldera
(agglomerate, pumice, trachyte,
tuff, basalt, vent agglomerate)

Shamsan Caldera
(trachyte & trachyandesite)

Main Cone
(trachybasalt, agglomerate,
rhyolite & trachyte)

Ma'alla
(rhyolite, trachyandesite,
agglomerate)

Gold Mohur Lavas
(trachybasalt & rhyolite)

Agglomerate

Source: K.G. Cox, I.G. Gass & D.I.J. Mallick (1969)
The evolution of the volcanoes of Aden
& Little Aden, South Arabia (Q.Jl geol. Soc. Lond)

ADEN VOLCANO

Clock Tower Hill

Tawahi

Ma'alla
(Alluvium)

Ras Qatam

Sirah Island

Front Bay

Amen Khal

Spion Kop

CRATER

Holkat Bay

Gold Mohur Bay

Tawila Gorge

pumice bed

Ra's Marshag

Conquest Bay

Ras Taih

Round Island Bay

Ra's Antuk

0   1 mile
0   2 km

The first inhabitants of Aden were surely fishermen. *The Periplus of the Erythrean Sea* says that 'nomads and fish-eaters' lived in the coastal villages east of Aden. Similarities have been detected between the double-ended surf boats (*sambuks*) seen in Mahrah and in Oman and the boats used in Buraika and Bir Fukum in Little Aden, some twelve kilometres across the broad bay to the west. In the past these had many oarsman and were often used to fish for shoals of tuna, mackerel and kingfish off Aden.

In the busy commercial Crater region of Aden, at the east end of the isthmus, a perfume retailer sells his goods to a multinational clientele.

The Tawila Tanks

The Tawila Tanks in Crater are the oldest construction in Aden, named after the gorge that cuts through the rocks beneath the eastern end of Jebel Shamsan. They are made up of a series of 18 cisterns carved out of solid rock, actually a volcanic trachyte, and dammed in places to take advantage of the underlying rock pattern. They were originally built to give some stability in water supply in an area where several years often pass without serious rainfall. They vary in size and depth, but capture and collect rain falling in the surrounding mountains. Their capacity is an estimated 90 million litres. Tanks are connected by a series of small aqueducts with the overflow from one tank passing to the next in a chain, transporting water right into the heart of Crater. They are believed to have been constructed while the control of Aden was in the hands of the Himyarites, sometime around the first century AD. But, since a port with the stature of Aden in ancient days would have needed an adequate amount of fresh water, it is possible that they existed before then in Sabaean times. Between 1856 and 1859 the tanks were cleaned out, restored and finally remodelled on the advice of Captain Haines and under the direction of the local political residents, Brigadier Cooghlan and Captain Playfair, in an attempt to make Aden completely independent of exterior sources for its water supply. Captain Playfair also published a memoir on the tanks as they existed in 1857 before their transformation. He described them as being built generally of stone and mud masonry, roughly plastered on the outside and beautifully coated by a thick coat of cream coloured stucco. 'Each tank has a smaller one in front of it, built for the purpose of retaining all earth and stones carried down by the torrent and permitting a pure stream of water to flow into the reservoir beyond.'

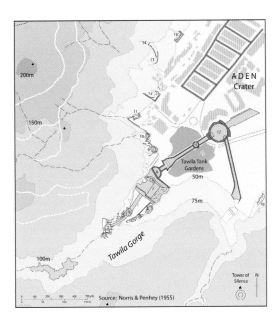

Tiny Sirah (*above middle*) gave shelter to those ships first using the Aden site as a victualling landfall in the early nineteenth century. It lies off the eastern coastline of the peninsula.

Today its prime activity is to serve as Aden's principal supplier of fish, seen landed *above bottom*.

The Islands of Yemen

Yemen has a number of islands spread like a string of pearls along its coast; from the numerous small, flat coral-fringed islands of the southern Red Sea (like Kamaran), which have developed on salt domes, to the smaller less common islands along the Gulf of Aden, most of which are close to the coast and are generally extinct volcanoes thrown up out of the sea during the late Neogene. Some are more distant, fragments of displaced continental crust, like the Socotran Archipelago, which became separated from the mainland about 27 million years ago.

Socotra (*Soqotra*)

Socotra is the largest in a small archipelago of four islands, which includes the Brothers (Samhah and Darsa) and Abd al-Kuri together with two rocky islets

Above, the beach at Qalansiyah and the distant tranquil Detwah lagoon, northwest Socotra.

Right, Young goat, Detwah, Qalansiyah, northwest Socotra.

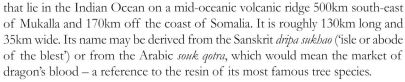

that lie in the Indian Ocean on a mid-oceanic volcanic ridge 500km south-east of Mukalla and 170km off the coast of Somalia. It is roughly 130km long and 35km wide. Its name may be derived from the Sanskrit *dripa sukhao* ('isle or abode of the blest') or from the Arabic *souk qotra*, which would mean the market of dragon's blood – a reference to the resin of its most famous tree species.

In antiquity it was known to the Greeks of the first century AD as the fabled Island of Dioscorida and described by Marco Polo in the late thirteenth century as the Island of Socotra – the market of the dragon's blood. Island of Bliss, Isle of Tranquillity, Island of Mists, Galapagos of the Indian Ocean and the Galapagos of the Arabian Peninsula are just some of the names which have been applied to the island over the centuries.

Strategically positioned near the main gateway to the Red Sea, Socotra has been famous since ancient times, and is mentioned in the oldest stories of the world. Gilgamesh of the Babylonian epic passed through the Waters of Death (the Bab al-Mandab straits) at the southern end of the Red Sea and came here to learn the secrets of immortality from a relative, known as Uta Napishtim (often referred to as a precursor of the biblical Noah). By the time of Abraham traders from Egypt, Africa, India and Arabia met here, while the ancient Egyptians knew Socotra as the Island of the Genie – the spirit of the sacred tree, whose gum they used for mummification, temple offerings and medicine. To the Greeks in the first century AD, it was famed for the phoenix, 'the Arabian bird' and locals believe that the oozing cinnabar-like resin of the dragon's blood tree is the result of an ancient myth of the combat between an elephant and a dragon, and the forces of life and death.

The Hadramaut kingdom traded here out of the port of Qana, near present-day Bir Ali on the Yemeni mainland, and later the Himyarites sailed here from Muza (Mocha) in the Red Sea. The island was on the main route for ships heading towards Aden from East Africa and India. (Pirates were a particular problem, but they too were known to put into Socotra to sell their goods.) Christianity came here, possibly with St Thomas, and by the time the monk Cosmas Indicopleustus arrived in the sixth century he found Christianity itself long established – alongside some idiosyncratic witchcraft.

In more recent centuries there has been an increasing interest in the island by European powers as an anchorage for ships, like the Portuguese Alphonso d'Alburquerque who built a fort and church here in 1507, but retired after failing to take Aden.

By 1834 the British wanted it for a coaling station. Captain Haines was sent to buy it from the sultan for £2,000, but despite his penury he refused to sell even an inch of the land, saying that it was a gift from the Almighty to the Mahras people. It eventually came under British protection in 1866, but was rarely visited by travellers except for the botanist Balfour in 1880 closely followed by the Riebeck expedition in the spring of 1881, to study the people and language. He was accompanied by the naturalist Schweinfurth, who also investigated the plants and conferred with Balfour. Dr Emil Riebeck is best remembered for the discovery of a new rock-forming mineral recovered from the Precambrian basement peralkaline granites of the central Haggier Range which bears his name to this day, described as 'Riebeckite' by Sauer in 1888, a well-known sodic amphibole and a common constituent of the best curling stones made from microgranite. A little later Theodore and Mabel Bent made a collection of plants whilst studying the archaeology in 1896-7.

Marco Polo elegantly summed up the island thus: 'The island of Socotra . . . produces beautiful cottons and other merchandise. There is an especially good trade in large salted fish, while the people live on rice, meat and milk.' The cottons may have gone, except for some kilm making, but the rest remains the same.

The island's population, which currently stands at 50,000, consists mostly of shepherds and fishermen who speak the unique Socotri dialect. The main population centres are towns along the north coast, such as Hadibu (*Hadibob*) (the principal administrative centre), Mouri, with its airport, Ghubbah, Qadheb and the western port of Qalansiyah. The coastal population represent quite a mix of backgrounds, consisting of Arabs (Hadrami and Gulf Arabs) who settled here on the islands over 3,000 years ago, as well as Greeks, Africans, Somalis, Mahri tribes, descendants of slaves, sailors, traders and shipwrecked seamen, and other races who have been migrating to the island since the twelfth century. There is also a Socotri-speaking bedouin population in the interior, who live in the hills, tending their cattle and goats. The variety is hardly surprising considering the island's long and chequered history.

The view from Jebel Skand, (c.1,600m) the highest mountain on the island, is breathtaki with the cloud base never far away in this eerie mountain-top world of white lichen-covered rocks and rugged proportions. Although Socotra is in the rain-bearing monsoon belt, it is predominantly the Haggi Mountains that attract the precipitation, with the result that their slopes are well vegetate and several of the streams perennial.

Their lives are substantially controlled by the two monsoon seasons which have such a profound effect on human activity and have historically contributed to the islands' isolation. These have helped to forge the islanders' cultural identity and their close harmony with their natural environment. It is not an easy life: water shortages, a restricted and monotonous diet, limited medical care, little formal schooling (although this is now being addressed) and historical isolation for nearly half of the year due to the monsoons. Some subsistence cultivation is practised, but this is minimal given the harsh climate, so the main land use is pastoralism.

The natural fresh water pool at D'kibkub, translated as the 'place of the star' perched high on a cliff above the northern coastal plain with its breathtaking views of the Arabian Sea. It is believed locally that it was a falling 'star' that caused the collapse of this end of the hanging valley. Homhil, north-eastern Socotra.

The south-west monsoons rage from April to October and bring extremely strong, hot and dry winds in from Africa. There is little precipitation and extreme desiccation during these months. The winter monsoon is less severe and blows in the opposite direction from the north-east, and the Indian subcontinent, bringing a little rain, and lasts from November until March.

Rainfall is always higher in the mountains than on the more arid coastal plains, but is sporadic, and there are some years when no rain falls at all. Nocturnal dew seems to be far more important to the water supply than monsoonal rain, especially in the high altitude mountain belt where the mountainous cloud zone provides ground water and running water for the entire island.

The coastal plains tend to be sub-desertic and are colonised by deciduous shrubs principally *Croton socotranus*, euphorbias, cucumber trees and *Ziziphus spina-christi,* but the foothills of the mountains contain a shrubby landscape with incense trees and more bizarre bottle-trunked trees. Socotra, it has to be said, is sparsely vegetated, but pockets of verdant vegetation survive the desiccating summer winds in sheltered valleys or in the high mountains. Due to the island's isolation, and the fact that human activity has been kept to a minimum, about 37 per cent of the flora is unique to the archipelago. Not surprisingly, the vegetation on the island is of great interest to botanists. Over 825 species of plant have now been recorded, and around 307 exist nowhere else in the world. This makes it one of the richest island floras in the world, and Socotra has even been described as the Galapagos of the Arabian Peninsula. The fauna on the island is equally remarkable, 90 per cent of its reptile species and 95 per cent of its land snail species do not occur anywhere else in the world. There are very few terrestrial mammals, most are introduced such as wild asses, camels, goats and sheep etc., although the bat *Rhinopoma sp.* and shrew *Suncus sp.* are possibly endemic.

Bottle trees resembling upturned root crops, and frankincense trees with their writhing shapes and characteristic peeling bark, have managed to gain a precarious foothold on this soilless karstified limestone slope. Upper Da'arho canyon, Central Socotra.

The ethnology and language of the island have been studied in depth by Dr Miranda Morris with special reference to the ethnobotany and how the islanders have used the plants on which they have depended for so long; recording the knowledge, passed down through generations, before it is lost through modernisation or change. This has been done in collaboration with The Royal Botanic Garden in Edinburgh (RBGE) who have had a long-standing relationship with the island ever since the visit to the island by their

Evergreen woodland is dominated by the dragon's blood tree *Dracaena cinnabari*, the island's otherworldly but iconic plant, growing on the limestone plateau above Wadi Da'arho.

Thousands of Socotran cormorants, *Phalacrocorax nigrogularis*, on the beach and in flotillas on the sea at remote Bander Shu'ub in Western Socotra.

curator Isaac Bayley Balfour in 1880, which resulted in the publication of the monumental work, the *Botany of Soqotra*. Since the early 1990s there has been a renewed acquaintance through the exacting taxonomic studies of Dr Tony Miller and his co-workers describing the islands' extraordinary flora, including the first specimen of a tiny carnivorous plant which grows on moist tree trunks in the higher reaches of the Haggier Mountains.

The catalogue of rare and peculiar drought-resistant plants that have developed is breathtaking, amongst them the bizarre upturned umbrella tree, *Dracaena sp.*, the flowering bottle tree, *Adenium ssp. sokotranum*, an endemic subspecies of a widespread African plant, but with a swollen rubbery leafless stem developed as an adaptation to the harsh conditions on the island. Water retentive bark and internal fluid recycling keep the plant cool. There are cucumber trees, *Dendrosicyos socotrana*, the only tree form in the cucumber-gourd-pumpkin family. These plants normally climb or creep along the ground.

There are frankincense and myrrh trees with their characteristic peeling bark, and also *Punica protopunica*, the wild relative of the pomegranate with its miniscule fruit, and the quite extraordinary dragon's blood tree, *Dracaena cinnabari*: so named after the deep-red liquid which exudes from its bark when scratched. This opaque, reddish-brown resinous juice is called gum dragon and was once much prized in a range of applications, including medicinal uses. It was highly regarded by Roman soldiers and gladiators as an ointment for disinfecting battle wounds and burns, and Stradivari, the violin maker, was renowned for using it in his varnishes. Today, the fresh resin is still exported to the mainland and is used in a number of medical applications and for the decoration of ceramics. In the thirteenth century it managed to find its way by a circuitous route across the oceans to China, along with another Socotran staple, whale ambergris, an indispensable constituent of cosmetics and perfume. Here the resin was known to the Chinese as blood's desiccate and was used to colour furniture lacquers. Over the centuries that followed this furniture was exported back into the western Indian Ocean together with tea and fine porcelain along the maritime Silk Road.

The dragon's blood tree, *Dracaena cinnabari*, is quite widespread in evergreen woodlands over the centre and east of the island and is the dominant tree in some areas. Some grow to over five hundred years old but are failing to regenerate and are listed as vulnerable. The tree grows best in areas affected

Wadi Danegan chocked with gigantic granite boulders from occasional flash floods, offers some protection from the desiccating winds. Here date palms are able to grow in a more sheltered situation.

by mists, low cloud and monsoon drizzle. A major cause of its decline is likely to be climate change, rather than goats on the island, which have already been there a long time. The achipelago appears to be gradually drying out, although drought amongst newly established individuals trying to gain a foothold is possibly the most serious cause (Jindřich Pavliš pers. comm). Growing some of the seedlings in a nursery situation is now being encouraged.

Plant species found here have evolved morphological and physiological adaptations to cope with the dry climate and fierce monsoonal winds. The bulbous and bizarre bottle tree, *Adenium ssp. socotranum*, has a special cell sap cycling within the swollen trunk which prevents overheating. The succulents display several morphological adaptations. Plant bodies are globular or columnar, with reduced surface areas decreasing transpiration. Glaceous waxy and silvery surfaces also help to reflect the sun's rays. Umbrella-shaped shrubs tend to bunch together in dense thickets, with all plants reaching the same height, a strategy which protects them from the worst effects of the winds.

Around the coasts there are large numbers of turtles which lay their eggs on the beaches near Ghubbah, spinning dolphins and some whales, in particular sperm whales. Marco Polo describes how sperm whales were caught here in the thirteenth century by fishermen from these islands using boats towing tuna bait soaked in brine. They were in search of ambergris, a peculiar fatty substance secreted in the intestines of the sperm whale but also found floating at sea or as a deposit on the shore. Because of its odour, it has been used in perfumes and pharmaceutical products over the centuries and it is still valuable today.

In an attempt to allow economic development on this unspoilt island where for centuries the islanders have lived in harmony with nature and preserved a unique, traditional way of life, the government, international companies and donor agencies are trying to ensure its survival by improving the lives of the people but at the same time conserving its globally significant biodiversity.

Organisations involved include the Yemeni government's Socotra Conservation and Development Programme (SCDP), which co-ordinates government and donor initiatives affecting the people, and has developed a zoning plan to ensure the survival of the main habitats and plants. Other organisations such as the Friends of Soqotra and the Socotra Conservation Fund contribute massively to this effort and are devoted to studying and conserving the island's resources.

The cucumber tree, *Dendrosicyos soqotranus*, is the type of vegetation for which Socotra is most renowned. Isolation has resulted in a high proportion of endemic species with beautiful and often bizarre adaptations.

Ecotourism

Socotra is a remote naturalist's paradise, which ecotourism offers a way of seeing. A formula of managed eco-friendly tourism has been developed to help generate income from visits to protected areas such as nature sanctuaries, national parks and areas of special botanical interest which encompass about 75 per cent of the total land area. This is an alternative Galapagos – an untouched, unique ecosystem – with pristine beaches and idyllic oases rarely visited by tourists.

The Diksam plateau (1) (see map on page 193) in the centre of the island is the base and starting point for trekking in the high Haggier Mountains with its stunning scenery and dragon's blood forests. From here the ascent of Jebel Skand (c.1600m/5250ft), currently the highest mountain on the island, is achievable, although strenuous, but is rewarded with spectacular views of the north coast and Haggier Range.

The high point, of any visit to this area is Wadi Da'arho, a deep water-cut canyon filled with massive rusty-coloured andesitic lavas, crammed full of luxuriant palm groves and freshwater pools for bathing and picknicking, high up on the Diksam plateau in the the shadow of the Haggier Mountains. This is dragon tree country, with trees over five hundred years old scattered about with random precision, like giant mushrooms, ancient relics of a flora frozen in time which has long since disappeared from mainland Africa and Arabia.

Wadi Da'arho, a deep water-cut canyon filled with rusty-coloured andesitic lavas and crammed full of luxuriant palm groves and freshwater pools used for bathing.

Traditional fishing boat or *huri* at Ras Dihamri Marine Reserve, an area of protected corals, on Socotra's north-eastern coast.

There is also Homhil (4) a peaceful protected area with special plants and succulent trees including mature stands of frankincense trees, *Boswellia*. It is remarkable for its natural fresh water pool at D'kibkub translated as the *'place of the star'* perched high on a cliff above the northern coastal plain with its breathtaking views of the Arabian Sea.

At Ras Dihamri Marine Protected Area (2) in northeast Socotra the seas of the Socotran Archipelago still remain in a largely pristine state with spectacular areas of hard and soft corals totaling over 283 species including branching Acropora. Corals form small, discrete communities here rather than true reef structures because of cool water upwelling during the south-west summer monsoons. They are home to around 730 species of coastal reef fish, with a complete range from groupers, snappers, butterfly fish, surgeonfish and puffer fish through to gigantic sunfish, predatory marlins, sailfish and basking sharks. Snorkelling and diving opportunities abound, providing the waters stay calm.

At Erher (5) further along the north coast near the eastern tip of the island is a remarkable stretch of beach. Hundred-foot storm dunes, carelessly tossed up against the cavernous limestone cliffs, attest to the strength and voracity of the prevailing onshore winds although they are constantly changing shape particularly during wet periods, when they may end up as the beach again. Warm spring water, piped down from the plateau is a welcome surprise.

The fruits of the sea on this stretch of coast are so abundant here that shoaling onshore waves literally toss their harvest of fish onto the shore to be picked up by the hordes of waiting waders or restless armies of scavenging

ghost crabs forever on the move. Massive sardine shoals stain the water purple and the nightly phosphorescent discharges in the sea produced by the agitation of small zooplankton give a spectacular nightly bioluminescent light show.

It is said that the seas around Socotra are teeming with so much fish that you only have to toss a hook in the water to be rewarded with one. Fishing here is seasonal from November to May as the monsoon winds from June to October make going to sea in a boat impossible. Fishing takes place in the morning if the weather permits, selling the surplus on to the local

Ghost crab mounds, and wading birds patrolling the beach at Erher in the hope of a catch. This beach on the north-eastern coast near the eastern tip of the island is notable for its hundred foot storm dunes.

co-operatives who pass it on to the fish factory on the outskirts of Hadibu for freezing and export to the rest of the Arab world and, more recently, Europe. Fishermen have the option of moving with their boats to Mukalla on the Yemeni mainland during this downtime or else resort to fishing from the shore or farming goats or dates. Some of the catches include massive fish such as marlin and sailfish as well as tuna and kingfish.

Erher has its own well-documented cave but further west in the coastal cliffs above Terbac village is the extraordinary Hoq cave complex which was discovered and protected by a team of Belgians led by Peter De Geest of the Socotran Karst Project (SKP) in the winter of 2000. Extraordinary stalactites and natural columns, and a history of ritual occupation all add to the fascination and interest of this three-kilometre long limestone cave complex which has been visited by people from around the first centuries AD, from east Africa, the Arabian mainland, western India, and Palmyra, as they plied the ancient sea trade routes.

In quite the most spectacular location a designated area has been set aside on the far west coast at Qalansiyah (3) beside the tranquil Detwah lagoon, one of Socotra's premier sites for wild birds and marine life along an expansive stretch of unspoilt sand. A trip by local fishing boat to Bandar Shu'ub, although bumpy, takes you to an even more remote beach around the coast, home to thousands of Socotran cormorants, *Phalacrocorax nigrogularis,* and spinning dolphins; to the accompaniment of aerial displays by brown boobies, *Sula leucogaster,* fishing by diving from great heights. This is a bird-watcher's paradise, with the island having by far the most native birds in the Middle East: 192 bird species, 44 of which breed on the islands, while 85 are regular migrants, including, sadly, a number of threatened species including the cormorant.

The extreme flatness and desolation of the Noged, the southern coastal plain, is remarkable, endless beaches stretch to infinity on the horizon. Here Amek beach (6) has been set aside for sorties into this barren inhospitable land. A strong longshore drift will entrain you and, even with the best intentions, you may not end up where you start from, as ghost crabs here in their thousands undermine the beach and visit at night. It was the Noged which took the brunt of the Indian Ocean Tsunami as it crashed into the East African coast, causing devastation to fishing communities and the loss of boats and houses in the area.

In 1998 the WWF designated Socotra as one of the 'Global 200' most important ecoregions on earth. By 2003 it was recognised as the first UNESCO Man and Biosphere Reserve in Yemen and as one of the best-preserved island ecosystems on the planet. It is hardly surprising, then, that in 2004 it was nominated as a potential World Heritage Site. Then at the 32nd session of the council on July 8, 2008 the Socotra Archipelago was finally added to UNESCO's World Heritage List, which now numbers 878 sites, as one of the 174 protected natural places in the world.

Bibliography

AITHIE, P (2006) *The Burning Ashes of Time: From Steamer Point to Tiger Bay, on the trail of seafaring Arabs*, Seren Publishing. Wales.

AL-'AMRI, H BIN A (1985) *The Yemen in the 18 & 19th centuries, a political & intellectual history*, Ithaca Press, London.

AL-HUBAISHI, A, AND MÜLLER-HOHENSTEIN, K (1984) *An Introduction to the Vegetation of Yemen: Ecological Basis, Floristic Composition, Human Influence*, Deutsche Gesellschaft für Technische Zusammenarbeit.

ALLFREE, P S (1967) *Hawks of the Hadhramaut*, Hale, London.

AMBRASEYS, N N, and MELVILLE, C P (1983) 'Seismicity of Yemen', *Nature*, 303, pp. 321-3.

AS-SARURI, M et al. (2007) *Geological Map of Yemen*, Ministry of Oil & Minerals, Petroleum Exploration & Production Authority (PEPA) website.

BALFOUR-PAUL, J (1997) *Indigo in the Arab World*, Curzon Press, Richmond.

BELHAVEN, MASTER OF (1949) *The Kingdom of Melchior—Adventure in South West Arabia*, John Murray, London.

BELHAVEN, LORD (1955) *The Uneven Road*, Murray, London.

BENOIST-MÉCHIN, J (1957) *Arabian Destiny*, Elek, London.

BENT, T AND M (1900/1994) *Southern Arabia*, Garnet, Reading.

BIDWELL, R (1983) *The Two Yemens*, Longman, London.

BISCH, J (1962) *Behind the Veil of Arabia*, Allen & Unwin, London.

BOTTING, D (1958) *Island of Dragon's Blood*, Hodder, London.

BOXHALL, P (1974) 'The Diary of a Mocha Coffee Agent', *Arabian Studies*, 1, pp. 102-18.

BRADLEY, C (1995) *Discovery Guide to Yemen*, Immel Publishing, London.

BROUWER, C G (1997) *Al-Mukha: Profile of a Yemeni seaport as sketched by servants of the Dutch East India Company (VOC) 1614-1640*, D'Fluyte Rarob, Amsterdam.

BURROWES, R D (1995) *Historical Dictionary of Yemen*, Scarecrow Press, Lanham, Maryland.

CHEUNG, C, DEVANTIER, L AND VAN DAMME, K (2006) *Socotra: A Natural History of the Islands and Their People*. Odessey Books. p.384.

COSTA, P M (1994) *Studies in Arabian Architecture, Variorum Collected Studies Series* CS 455, Variorum, Ashgate Publishing Ltd, Aldershot.

COX, K G, GASS I G, & MALLICK D I J (1969) 'The evolution of the volcanoes of Aden and little Aden, South Arabia', *Quarterly Journal of the Geological Society*, London, 124, pp. 283-308.
(1977) 'The Western part of the Shuqra volcanic field, South Yemen', Lithos, 10, pp 185-91.

DAMLUJI, S S (1991) *A Yemen Reality—Architecture Sculptured in Mud and Stone*, Garnet, Reading.

DAMLUJI, S S (1992) *The Valley of Mud Brick Architecture—Shibam, Tarim and Wadi Hadramut*, Garnet Publishing, Reading.

DAUM, W (1987) *Yemen: 3000 years of Art and Civilisation in Arabia Felix*, Pinguin-Verlag, Innsbruck; Umschau-Verlag, Frankfurt/Main.

DOE, B (1971) *Southern Arabia*, Thames and Hudson, London.

DORSKY, S (1986) *Women of Amran—A Middle Eastern Ethnographic Study*, University of Utah, Salt Lake City.

FREITAG, U, AND CLARENCE-SMITH W G (eds) *Hadhrami Traders, Scholars and Statesmen in the Indian Ocean, 1750s to1960s, Social, Economic, and Political Studies of the Middle East and Asia.*

GAVIN, R J (1975) *Aden under British Rule 1839-1967*, Hurst, London.

GIBSON, M AND WILKINSON, T J (1993-6) *Oriental Institute Archaeological and Environmental Investigation of Yemeni Terraced Agriculture*, University of Chicago Oriental Institute Investigations in Yemen Annual Reports, 1993-4, 1994-5 and 1995-6.

GIOVANNUCCI, D et al. (2005) *Moving Yemen coffee forward — assessment of the coffee industry in Yemen to sustainably improve incomes and expand trade.* USAID Report.

HÄMÄLINEN, P (1991) *Yemen: A Travel Survival Kit*, Lonely Planet, Australia.

HANSEN, T (1964) *Arabia Felix — The Danish Expedition of 1761-1767*, Collins, London.

HARRIS, W B (1893) *A Journey Through Yemen and Some General Remarks upon That Country*, Blackwood, Edinburgh and London.

HÉBERT, J (1989) *Yemen — Invitation to a Voyage in Arabia Felix*, Azal, Ottawa.

HELFRITZ, H (1935) *Land Without Shade*, Hurst & Blackett, London.

HINCKINBOTHAM, SIR T (1958) *Aden*, Constable, London.

INGRAMS, H (1942) *Arabia and the Isles*, John Murray, London.

JENNER, M (1983) *Yemen Rediscovered*, Longman, London and New York.

JOHNSTON, C H (1964) *The View from Steamer Point*, Collins, London.

KIERNAN, R H (1937) *The Unveiling of Arabia — the Story of Arabian Travel and Discovery*, Harrap, London.

KLORMAN, B-Z E (1997) *The Jews of Yemen in the Nineteenth Century — A Portrait of a Messianic Community*, E J Brill, Leiden.

KNEES, S G AND MILLER, A G (eds) (2006) *Flora of the Socotra Archipelago Illustrated Key.* A G Miller, M. Morris, D, Alexander and R Atkinson.

KOUR, Z H (1981) *The History of Aden*, Frank Cass, London.

LEWCOCK, R (1986) *Wadi Hadramawt and the Walled City of Shibam*, UNESCO, Paris. (1986) *The Old Walled City of San'a'*, UNESCO, Paris.

LUNT, J (1966) *The Barren Rocks of Aden*, Herbert Jenkins, London.

MACKINTOSH-SMITH, T (1997) *Yemen: Travels in Dictionary Land*, John Murray, London.

MACRO, E (1968) *Yemen and the Western World*, Hurst, London.

DE MAIGRET, A (2001) *Arabia Felix — An exploration of the archaeological history of Yemen*, Stacey International, London.

MENELEY, A (1996) Tournaments of Value: Sociability and Hierarchy in a Yemeni Town, *Anthropological Horizons 9*, University of Toronto.

MILLER, A G and Cope, T A (1996) *Flora of the Arabian Peninsula and Socotra* – Vol 1, Edinburgh University Press.

MILLER, A G and Morris, M (2004) *Ethnoflora of the Soqotra Archipelago*. Royal Botanical Garden Edinburgh.

MILLER, A G and Morris, M et al., (2006) *Socotra — Land of the Dragon's Blood Tree.* Royal Botanical Gardens, Edinburgh.

VAN DER MEULEN, D (1947) *Aden to the Hadramaut: A Journey in South Arabia*, John Murray, London. (1947) *Faces in Shem*, John Murray, London.

VAN DER MEULEN, D, AND VON WEISSMANN, H (1964) *Hadramaut — Some of its Mysteries Unveiled*, E J Brill, Leiden.

NORRIS, H T AND PENHEY, F W (1955) *An Archaeological and Historical Survey of the Aden Tanks*, Aden Government Press, Aden.

OLSON, D AND DINERSTEIN, E (1998) *The Global 200: a representation approach to conserving the earth's most biologically valuable regions.* Conservation Biology 12, pp.502-515.

PHILBY, H ST JOHN (1939) *Sheba's Daughters: Being a record of travel in Southern Arabia,* Methuen, London.

PHILLIPS, W (1955) *Qataban and Sheba — Exploring Ancient Kingdoms on the Biblical Spice Routes of Arabia,* Gollancz, London.

PIEPENBURG, F (1983) *Traveller's Guide to Yemen,* Yemen Tourist Company, Sana'a.

POLO, M (1984) *The Travels of Marco Polo — A modern translation by Teresa Waugh from the Italian by Maria Bellonci,* Sidgwick & Jackson, London.

POSEY, S (1994) *Yemeni Pottery,* British Museum Press, London.

RAIKES, R L (1977) *Ma'rib Dam.* Antiquity 51, pp.239-240.

ROBINSON, J B D (1993) *Coffee in Yemen — A Practical Guide: Rural Development Project Al-Mahwit Province.* Klaus Schwarz Verlag, Berlin, p.87.

SCOTT, H (1975) *In the High Yemen,* AMS Press, New York.

SERJEANT, R B (1976) *South Arabian Hunt,* Luzac & Co, London.

SERJEANT, R B, AND LEWCOCK, R (eds) (1983) *San'a' an Arabian Islamic City,* World of Islam Festival Trust, London.

SMITH, C (1982) 'Kaukaban: Some of its History', *Arabian Studies 6,* pp. 35-50.

SMITH, G R (compiler) (1984) *The Yemens — Yemen Arab Republic and the People's Democratic Republic of Yemen,* World Bibliographical Series, vol 50, Clio Press, Oxford.

SMITH, G REX, SERJEANT, R B (ed) SMITH, G REX (1996) *Society and Trade in South Arabia Variorum,* Ashgate, Aldershot.

STARK, F (1936) *The Southern Gates of Arabia — A Journey in the Hadhramaut,* John Murray, London.

(1939) *Seen in the Hadhramaut,* John Murray, London.

(1940) *A Winter in Arabia,* John Murray, London.

(1947) *East is West,* John Murray, London.

(1953) *The Coast of Incense,* John Murray, London.

STONE, F (1985) *Studies on the Tihama,* Longman, London.

TYABJI, R AND C TINTSTMAN (eds) (1995) *Welcome to Yemen,* a UNICEF Guide, Horizons Printing, Sana'a.

VARANDA, F (1981) Art of Building in Yemen, Art and Archaeology, Research Papers, London.

VARISCO, D M (1994) *Medieval Agriculture and Islamic Science: The Almanac of a Yemeni Sultan.* University of Washington Press, Seattle and London, p.349.

VARISCO, D M (1996) 'Water Sources and Traditional Irrigation in Yemen', *New Arabian Studies 3,* University of Exeter Press.

VOGEL, D (ed) (1997) Insight Guides: Yemen, Apa, Hong Kong.

WALD, P (1996) *Yemen,* Pallas Guides, London.

WEIR, S (1985) *Qat in Yemen,* British Museum, London.

WOOD, T G, LAMB, R W AND BEDNARZIK, M (1986) *Two Species of Microtermes* (Isoptera, Termitidae, Macrotermitinae) *from the Arabian Peninsula',* Journal of Natural History 20, pp.165-82.

Index